TRIAL PREP FOR PARALEGALS

EFFECTIVE CASE MANAGEMENT AND SUPPORT TO ATTORNEYS IN PREPARATION FOR TRIAL

TRIAL PREP FOR PARALEGALS

EFFECTIVE CASE MANAGEMENT AND SUPPORT TO ATTORNEYS IN PREPARATION FOR TRIAL

MICHAEL L. COYNE
AND
URSULA FURI-PERRY

NATIONAL INSTITUTE FOR TRIAL ADVOCACY

Reprint Permission

National Institute for Trial Advocacy
361 Centennial Parkway, Suite 220
Louisville, CO 80027
Phone: (800) 225-6482
Fax: (720) 890-7069
E-mail: permissions@nita.org

Library of Congress Cataloging-in-Publication Data
Coyne, Michael L.
  Trial prep for paralegals : effective case management and support to attorneys in preparation for trial / Michael L. Coyne and Ursula Furi-Perry.
      p. cm.
  ISBN 978-1-60156-084-1
  1. Pre-trial procedure--United States. 2. Legal assistants--United States.
I. Furi-Perry, Ursula. II. Title.
  KF8900.C69 2009
  347.73'72--dc22

                                     2009018461

ISBN 978-1-60156-084-1
FBA 1084
12 11 10 09   10 9 8 7 6 5 4 3 2 1
Printed in the United States of America

CONTENTS

ACKNOWLEDGMENTS

A heartfelt thanks to the publishing and editing team at the National Institute for Trial Advocacy for all of its hard work on this book.

This book contains much advice and hopefully a bit of wisdom from the many mentors, family members, friends, colleagues, and students who helped along the way in the development of making us better lawyers, listeners, and counselors.

INTRODUCTION

Behind every great trial lawyer is a team of great lawyers and non-attorney legal staff helping prepare for trial. Paralegals, legal assistants, and other nonlawyers play an invaluable role in trial preparation, whether through organizing the attorney's trial notebook, gathering evidence and information, assisting with jury selection, or corresponding with the client and opposing counsel.

Trial Prep for Paralegals is a thorough, readable, and comprehensive handbook, focusing on the practical skills and substantive knowledge litigation paralegals need as well as the paralegal's role in the trial process. This book provides valuable tips about the litigation paralegal's many job functions: fact gathering; interviewing; investigation; case file organization and maintenance; witness coordination; exhibit preparation and maintenance; and correspondence.

The first part of the book focuses on substantive learning, with an overview of the litigation process, and the rules of civil procedure and evidence. The second part details practical tips for real-life application, from organizing war rooms to putting together trial notebooks. The third part offers tips and advice on working together with the rest of the trial team.

The following are some of the key features of this book:

- Attorney-paralegal team perspectives
- Organizational tips
- Tips for interviewing and investigation
- Tips for mastering discovery, including e-discovery
- Tips for assisting with testimonial evidence
- Tips for mastering trial technology
- Case management strategies
- Trial prep checklists
- Discussion questions
- Chapter glossaries

Trial attorneys rely on their legal staff, who must understand the litigation process, the paralegal's role at trial, and the assistance paralegals need to provide in trial preparation—litigation paralegals must be able to hit the ground running. Hence, the attorney-paralegal team will benefit from *Trial Prep for Paralegals*, a book that spells out the most effective ways for legal staff to assist attorneys before and during trial. Use this book as a resource guide to effectively and efficiently assist your attorney in preparation for trial.

PART I
SUBSTANTIVE LEARNING

LITIGATION OVERVIEW

This chapter provides an overview of litigation concepts, explaining the litigation process, jurisdiction of the courts, and the relevant rules of procedure. Here, you'll learn the basic procedural and substantive concepts governing litigation, while in subsequent chapters, you'll learn their practical applications on the job.

CHAPTER OVERVIEW

By the end of this chapter, you should be familiar with

- the litigation process and its alternatives;
- sources of legal authority;
- jurisdiction and its related concepts;
- pleadings, affirmative defenses, and service of process;
- the discovery process;
- civil remedies;
- pretrial, trial, and posttrial motions;
- the appellate process;
- relevant rules of the Federal Rules of Civil Procedure.

INTRODUCTION TO THE LITIGATION PROCESS

Litigation is the process of filing a case in court and pursuing that controversy through the court system for resolution. Though courts can hear civil, criminal, and even administrative cases, the majority of litigation paralegals work on civil matters—disputes between private persons or entities. Civil lawsuits can center around a wide variety of subjects:

- Business disputes, such as matters involving intellectual property, unfair competition, wrongful termination, or employment discrimination;

- Torts, which are civil wrongs committed either intentionally (such as assault or battery), negligently (such as an accident or personal injury), or under strict liability (such as injury from a wild animal that is kept on another person's property, or product liability claims for defective, inherently unsafe products);

- Contractual claims, such as breach of contract or breach of a fiduciary duty;

- Property disputes, such as suits based on a real estate transaction and boundary or title controversies.

The plaintiff—the party who initiates the litigation—may seek several types of remedies from the defendant, the party against whom the suit is brought. Though most suits involve money damages, a plaintiff may also seek equitable remedies, such as an injunction, which prevents a party from doing something, or specific performance, which compels a party to perform in accordance with the terms of a contract.

During any lawsuit, the court will apply both substantive and procedural law to resolve the case. Substantive law governs the rights and responsibilities of the parties—which is the subject matter of a suit—and may include case law, statutory law, administrative regulations and decisions, constitutional law, ordinances and other local laws, and even international laws. By contrast, procedural law governs the method of resolving a dispute in court and any rules that address the litigation process. Think of it in terms of a card game: each game involves a different makeup of cards, but the basic rules of play stay the same; similarly, in court, the substantive subject matter changes from one case to another, but the procedural rules governing suits are constant. In federal court, the Federal Rules of Civil Procedure (FRCP) govern civil suits. In turn, all states have their own rules of civil procedure to follow in their courts. Though the rules mentioned in this book are based on the federal rules, you will find that most states have adopted the federal rules with few changes. That isn't to say, of course, that you shouldn't research the applicable procedural rules of your jurisdiction—you should!

SETTLEMENT AND OTHER METHODS OF ALTERNATIVE DISPUTE RESOLUTION

The vast majority of civil controversies are not litigated in court to a jury verdict—they are most often settled when, before a jury verdict, the parties reach an agreement that's mutually acceptable outside of court. Paralegals can play an essential part in the settlement process. For example, while trial attorneys conduct settlement discussions on their clients' behalf, paralegals may assist with fact gathering and verification, computation of damages, correspondence, and client comfort. A paralegal may also help the attorney put together a settlement brochure or settlement workup: a document that summarizes for the other side all of the major facts supporting the client's case and damages up to the present.

In addition to settlement, there are various forms of alternative dispute resolution that help the two parties keep the case out of court. Commonly called ADR, alternative dispute resolution encompasses many different nonjudicial dispute resolution processes in which a neutral person attempts to help resolve the parties' dispute. The principal methods of ADR are the following:

- **Arbitration** is the process in which an impartial panel or single arbitrator hears arguments, conducts hearings, and issues a decision on the dispute. The arbitrator's decision can be either binding or nonbinding, depending on the parties' agreement.

- **Early neutral evaluation** is a process in which the parties agree early in the process to submit their facts in brief form to an impartial person who will evaluate the matter and provide an opinion regarding the likely outcome.

- **Collaborative practice** is a voluntary process used to facilitate the resolution of the dispute. All participants, including the lawyers, agree to focus on negotiation and settlement rather than litigation. It generally provides for the disclosure of all information while emphasizing collaborative, cooperative, and "win-win" based negotiation.

- **Conciliation** is a voluntary process in which the parties and trained conciliator discuss the matter and consider solutions to the dispute in order to reach an agreement. The conciliator leads the parties through the dispute resolution process. The conciliator does not render a decision on the dispute, but attempts to empower the parties to reach a mutually acceptable solution.

- **Mediation** is a voluntary process in which a neutral expert trained in dispute resolution discusses the dispute with the parties and works with them to reach a mutually acceptable settlement. A mediator will often identify the areas of disagreement and the strengths and weaknesses of each side, and then use that information to help the parties narrow the areas of disagreement to reach an agreement satisfactory to both sides.

- **Minitrial** is a voluntary settlement process in which the parties present a summary of their evidence and arguments to a neutral expert and then meet with that expert to discuss the value and possible settlement of the case.

- **Private judging** is a minitrial that generally takes place before a retired judge who makes a decision regarding what would happen if the matter were tried. This aids the parties in evaluating the case for and achieving a settlement.

- **Summary jury trial** is a voluntary nonbinding jury determination in which the parties present a summary of their evidence and arguments to a jury, which may come from the court's potential jury venire or be privately arranged. The "jury" then deliberates and returns a decision on the dispute. This determination and discussion of the case with these private jurors is helpful to the parties as they try to mediate their dispute.

Alternative dispute resolution is now often the favored method of dispute resolution, as it is a faster, more economical, and often more amicable method of resolving disputes than litigation. Paralegals assist their attorneys throughout the alternative dispute resolution process as much as they assist in all stages of the litigation process.

SOURCES OF LEGAL AUTHORITY

Adjudication of a case is largely determined by the doctrine of precedence: when a new case is brought, the court looks to past case law and other existing legal authority to decide that case. Under the doctrine of precedence, an issue that was decided one way in a past case should be similarly decided in the current case. In rare cases, the court may choose to change the law on an issue and decline to follow past precedent. In some instances, you may even encounter a case of first impression—an issue for which there is no precedent in your jurisdiction; in those cases, you look for support for your case from decisions in other jurisdictions.

A court may apply both common law (court opinions) and enacted law (statutes, constitutions, or ordinances) in determining the outcome of a case. Sources of legal authority derive from all three branches of government—for example, the legislature enacts statutes; the courts issue opinions; and administrative agencies under the executive branch formulate administrative regulations. Those three branches operate at three levels of government: federal, state, and local or municipal.

When you are conducting legal research, you will find both primary and secondary sources of authority. Primary authority consists of laws—cases, statutes, ordinances, regulations, the United States Constitution and state constitutions. Secondary authority is not law; rather, its function is to explain, summarize, or otherwise help you understand the law. Some examples of secondary authority include treatises, law review articles and notes, legal periodicals, continuing legal education materials, and form books.

It is important not only to know the various sources of legal authority that a court may apply when deciding a case, but also to understand their effect on the court's decision making. Secondary authority may only be used persuasively—though you might present it to a court to sway the jury or judge in one direction, secondary authority will never be mandatory or binding on a court. Only primary authority may be binding. A past case will be binding if it was decided by a higher court in the same jurisdiction. For example, if you bring suit in a district court in your state, then a past case from your state's appellate court will serve as binding authority on your court. However, a past case from another state will only be persuasive, not binding.

Now that you understand the different sources of legal authority a court may use to decide a case, it is time to choose the court in which you will file your case.

Jurisdiction

Before you file your case, you must decide on the proper forum—the right court in which to bring your suit. You must establish the court's jurisdiction, which is the power of the court to decide the case and bind the parties to its judgment. To do so, you will have to establish three matters to ensure that the court can properly hear the matter: subject matter jurisdiction, personal jurisdiction, and venue.

Subject Matter Jurisdiction

Subject matter jurisdiction is the power of the court over the controversy—the type of case you are bringing. The power to hear controversies derives from the Constitution and various federal and state statutes. Without subject matter jurisdiction, any judgment that the court renders is void; in fact, lack of subject matter jurisdiction can be raised as a defense by anyone at any time during the proceedings.

Subject matter jurisdiction determines whether your case should be brought in federal or state court. There are several ways to get through the door at the federal courthouse. Federal courts have subject matter jurisdiction of all civil actions arising under the Constitution and laws or treaties of the United States regardless of the amount in controversy. Federal courts also have jurisdiction over controversies involving state law if there is diversity of citizenship between the defendant(s) and plaintiff(s). In order to establish diversity jurisdiction, no plaintiff can be from the same state as any defendant, and the claim must be likely to exceed $75,000 in damages.

Take, for example, a car accident between a plaintiff from Massachusetts and a defendant from California. Because no plaintiff in that case is from the same state as any defendant, the case could be brought in federal court as long as the damages are likely to exceed $75,000. So, even though there is no violation of federal law, a federal court could decide that case, even though the subject matter—the law of negligence—is ordinarily an issue reserved for state law and resolved in a state court. For the purposes of diversity of citizenship jurisdiction, corporations are citizens of both their state of incorporation and the state in which they have their principal place of business.

The subject matter jurisdiction for a violation of law may be either concurrent or exclusive. Concurrent jurisdiction means the case may be brought in either federal or state court, with the choice originally left up to the plaintiff. Exclusive jurisdiction means the action must be brought in either federal or state court—for example, federal courts have exclusive jurisdiction over some federal issues, such as bankruptcy cases, while state courts have exclusive jurisdiction over certain issues of state law, including divorce actions and other family law matters.

You have just learned that generally, federal issues of law are litigated in federal court, while state issues are resolved by a state court. But what if your case includes both federal and state issues? The doctrine of supplemental jurisdiction provides jurisdiction over other claims that arise from the same set of operative facts as the principal claim asserted in federal court. Under that doctrine, you can bring suit in federal court, and the court will have the authority to decide both the federal and the state issues. Likewise, those federal issues that are not within the exclusive jurisdiction of the federal court can be brought with related state claims in state court, and the state court will then have the ability to resolve both federal and state claims.

Suppose that either a state court or a federal court has subject matter jurisdiction over a case. The choice between federal and state court initially belongs to the plaintiff. The plaintiff is the "master of her complaint" and therefore decides on the forum court. However, if the suit could have been brought in federal court but was brought in state court, the defendant still has a procedural move at his or her disposal. Removal jurisdiction provides the defendant the right to remove an action from state court to federal court if the action could have otherwise been brought in federal court, unless the basis for removal is diversity jurisdiction, and the defendant resides in the state where the suit was entered.

Personal Jurisdiction

Personal jurisdiction is the power of the court to bind the defendant to any judgment it renders. It is obtained by establishing the defendant's minimum contacts within the jurisdiction such that the court's exercise of jurisdiction is reasonable—whether it is reasonable to expect the defendant to be sued and have to answer a suit in the forum state. With personal jurisdiction, the courts look at whether it was foreseeable that the defendant could expect being hailed into court in that jurisdiction; whether the defendant's activity within the forum was systematic and continuous; and what level of activity the defendant had in the forum state.

Some examples of activities that can establish minimum contacts—and therefore establish personal jurisdiction—include residence in a state, doing business in a state, or consenting to the exercise of jurisdiction in a contract (especially common in Internet-related contracts). In some cases, though, the court has found sufficient minimum contacts through a whole host of small contacts. In one franchise case involving Burger King, the court looked at the choice of law provision within the contract, visits to the forum state for training, the defendants' phone contacts to the forum state, and the anticipated contractual payments to the forum state, and held that the requisite minimum contacts were established for the defendants in the forum state.[1]

An individual who is personally served in the forum state—physically present at the time of service, even for a short visit—is subject to personal jurisdiction in that state. Jurisdiction may even be established through the defendant's ownership of property when the property is the focus of the dispute; this is called in rem jurisdiction.

Personal jurisdiction may be waived and conferred by the consent of the defendant. The defendant confers personal jurisdiction upon the court by failing to raise it, and therefore waiving any objection to it, in his initial reply. By failing to object to lack of personal jurisdiction in his first motion or pleading, the defendant has effectively consented to the court's power to bind him to its judgment.

Venue

Venue refers to the proper judicial district in which to bring the action. The forum court should be a convenient place to try the case based on where the witnesses can be seated and the evidence located. Like personal jurisdiction, improper venue may be waived and can be conferred by consent if not raised initially.

In federal court, venue is determined by asking where a substantial part of the cause of action arose or where the defendant resides. If you are involved in business litigation, note that a corporation resides wherever it has established sufficient minimum contacts for the exercise of personal jurisdiction. Some matters, like disputes against federal or state agencies, involve specific venue granting statutes—so, research issues of venue to see what the requirements are where you intend to file suit. In state court, venue is determined by asking where the cause of action arose or where the plaintiff or the defendant is located.

The defendant may file a motion to transfer the case on the basis of forum non conveniens—the court will weigh whether there is a more convenient place to try the case based upon the location of the evidence, witnesses, and the forum's interest in resolving the dispute. The plaintiff's choice of forum, however, is given a great deal of consideration in resolving motions to transfer on the basis of a forum non conveniens argument.

---

1. Burger King v. Rudzewicz, 471 U.S. 462 (1985).

PLEADINGS

Now that you have established the court's jurisdiction in your choice of forum, it is time to file your case on behalf of your client, the plaintiff. The litigation begins with the parties' filing of pleadings, which are the initial documents exchanged between the parties that set out the parties' positions.

- Complaint—the plaintiff files a complaint, along with all applicable filing fees, to start off the litigation. The complaint must state a prima facie cause of action in order to withstand a motion to dismiss; this means that in your complaint, you must show that there has been a violation of the law and that your client's rights have been affected by that violation. According to FRCP 8, complaints should contain statements of fact, not conclusions of law, and they should state the facts in a clear and concise manner. Most states follow notice pleading, where the plaintiff is only required to put the other side on notice of what happened. If your client wants a jury trial, it is good practice for the complaint to contain a jury trial demand—under FRCP 38, if you do not demand a jury trial, you will waive your rights to one. You should also consult the local court rules for any other format or content requirements for pleadings filed in that forum. After the complaint is filed, the plaintiff must serve the defendant with process. The Due Process Clause of the U.S. Constitution requires that the defendant be provided with reasonable notice and the opportunity to be heard prior to the award of judgment. Rule 4 provides the mechanics for effectuating service of process that is consistent with the requirements of the Due Process Clause. State long-arm statutes and the like provide a manner of giving notice to defendants who are absent from the forum state's jurisdiction, allowing process to extend beyond the state's borders.

- Answer—in response to the complaint, the defendant may file either a motion to dismiss or an answer to the plaintiff's allegations in the complaint. If the defendant fails to respond within the statutory time allotted, the plaintiff may obtain a default judgment under FRCP 55. An answer is a responsive pleading that requires the defendant to answer the complaint in a clear and concise manner, either admitting or denying the allegations in the complaint. In addition, the defendant may note any affirmative defenses under Rule 8(c). Some of the most common affirmative defenses include statute of limitations (the applicable time period to bring this cause of action has elapsed); laches (the plaintiff has delayed asserting his rights, which has caused prejudice to the other side); estoppel (a position has been taken earlier upon which the opposition has relied and therefore, the plaintiff is bound to that earlier position); and res judicata and collateral estoppel (defenses that assert that these same claims or issues have been previously litigated and therefore cannot be relitigated.) The defendant is required to consolidate affirmative defenses in the initial answer or risk waiving them.

- Counterclaims and cross-claims—the defendant may also file counterclaims and cross-claims. Counterclaims are causes of action the defendant asserts toward the plaintiff under FRCP 13. Counterclaims are either *compulsory,* meaning they arise from the same set of facts as the plaintiff's principal claim; or permissive, meaning they arise from a different set of facts as the principal claim. Compulsory counterclaims must be brought in response to the principal claim or be forever lost. Because they arise from the same common nucleus of operative fact as the principal claim, there is no need for a separate basis for jurisdiction. Permissive counterclaims, however, do need a separate basis for jurisdiction. In some cases, the plaintiff may be required to file a responsive pleading called a reply in response to the defendant's counter-claim. Cross-claims are causes of action asserted between codefendants who are already a party to the litigation.

OTHER CONSIDERATIONS ABOUT THE PARTIES AND THEIR PLEADINGS

There are some other important considerations to keep in mind regarding the parties and their pleadings:

- FRCP 19, 20, 21, and 22 deal with joinder of the parties and state that all parties must be properly named—in fact, the case can be dismissed for failure to join an indispensable party. You must address issues of standing and legal responsibility: Have someone's legal rights been affected so that the person has a cause of action? Are all necessary defendants named in the case?

- Rule 23 covers class action suits. Where a large group of people have been injured as a result of common questions of law or fact, they can sue collectively to obtain relief. The named representative of the class must be capable of adequately representing the interests of the class members, and the class representative's injury must fairly and typically represent the injury that the class has suffered.

- Intervenors under Rule 24 are individuals who are not named in the suit but have a legal interest in the suit, so they seek the court's permission to become a party to the action.

- Impleaders or third-party practice involves the defendant seeking to assert claims against parties not yet present but who may be responsible to the defendant for all or a portion of any judgment.

- Under FCRP 15 pleadings can be amended after they are filed. A complaint may be amended without leave of the court before an answer is filed; afterwards, the court's leave is required. Pursuant to the rules, leave to amend should be freely given.

- Finally, there is one more important rule to consult with any pleading or other filing you may assert on behalf of a client. Rule 11 describes the good-faith requirement of all attorneys who sign pleadings. In every pleading that you file on your client's behalf, the attorney certifies to the court that she has read the pleading, understands it, and made an investigation into the facts; that the pleading is based on existing law or a good-faith belief in reversal of existing law; that it is not interposed for any improper purpose, such as delay or harassment; and that the attorney believes that it is a meritorious pleading. Violation of Rule 11 may result in attorney sanctions.

DISCOVERY

Once the pleadings are all filed, discovery, the formal exchange of information between the parties, shortly begins. The federal rules, and some state rules as well, require a disclosure of information before formal discovery can begin. The discovery process is in place to ensure a more level playing field: it gives both sides the opportunity to receive and examine information in the other's possession that is relevant to the litigation so that there are no *Law & Order*-style surprises at trial. The sharing of relevant discoverable information that is not privileged is paramount under the rules and may facilitate a speedier resolution to the matter.

There are five methods by which information can be discovered:

- Depositions—under FRCP 30, a party or witness—whom we call the deponent or person being deposed—is asked to answer oral or written questions under oath. Depositions are the most common form of discovery, and often paralegals and lawyers spend a significant amount of time preparing for and assisting with depositions. Parties receive notice of the deposition, while nonparties are served with a subpoena under Rule 45, along with the notice of deposition, to compel their attendance. The deponent may be served with a subpoena duces tecum, which compels the witness to bring documents or other things to the deposition. Attorneys examine and may cross-examine the witness during a deposition. The deponent's testimony is preserved by audio, video, or stenography. While more costly, a video deposition may be the best method for preserving and presenting to the jury the testimony of an important witness.

- Interrogatories—under Rule 33 a party sends a set of written questions to the opposing party for his written responses. Interrogatories are answered under oath and subject to the penalties of perjury.

- Requests for the production of documents—under Rule 34 one side asks the other side to produce pertinent documents or items that may be the subject of the dispute, such as a defective product or invention.

- Requests for admissions—under Rule 36 one party sends a set of factual statements to the opposing party and asks the opposing party to either admit or deny each statement. If the opposing party fails to admit to requests properly made under Rule 36, then that party may bear the cost of producing that proof.

- Requests for physical or mental examination—under Rule 35 one party asks another to submit to an examination when that person's mental or physical condition is in issue. These requests are limited to parties and agents of parties.

The scope of discovery is established by Rule 26 (b)(1):

> Parties may obtain discovery regarding any nonprivileged matter that is relevant to any party's claim or defense—including the existence, description, nature, custody, condition, and location of any documents or other tangible things and the identity and location of persons who know of any discoverable matter. For good cause, the court may order discovery of any matter relevant to the subject matter involved in the action. Relevant information need not be admissible at the trial if the discovery appears reasonably calculated to lead to the discovery of admissible evidence.

If relevant information is formally requested during the discovery process, it must be provided unless there is a valid reason for not turning over the information. For example, information may be privileged. This means it is confidential and only certain people have the right to receive it, such as information shared under the attorney-client privilege.

Suppose that, at your attorney's request, you interview a client and then write a memorandum to the attorney summarizing the details of your interview. The memorandum you prepared will be protected by the attorney-client privilege—a privilege that applies to information shared by the client in anticipation of litigation, which are confidential communications between the attorney and the client. The memorandum will not be discoverable, which means you will not have to turn it over to the opposing party. Privilege can be waived through the disclosure of information, so always carefully review discovery information with your attorney before releasing any information on your own.

Generally, though, relevant information must be turned over to the other side if it is requested during discovery. If a party unjustly refuses to comply with a discovery request, the other party may file a motion to compel compliance with discovery. The court may then order compliance. If the noncompliant party still refuses to turn information over, the court may impose a wide range of sanctions under Rule

37, ranging from simple fines to preclusion from producing certain information or contesting certain issues, all the way to an adverse judgment. Rule 37 gives teeth to the requirement that parties should comply with all proper discovery requests. Compliance with discovery is taken so seriously that sanctions for noncompliance can be assessed on the client, the attorney, and even the law firm!

PRETRIAL AND TRIAL MOTIONS

A party may file a motion, a petition to the court, on a variety of different legal issues. The following are three important motions where a party asks the court to scrutinize the sufficiency of his opponent's case.

Motion to Dismiss

The defendant may file a motion to dismiss the plaintiff's case for various reasons under FRCP 12: lack of subject matter jurisdiction; lack of personal jurisdiction; improper venue; failure to join an indispensable party; misnomer of a party; improper service of process; or insufficient process. In addition, the defendant may file a motion to dismiss under Rule 12(b)(6), asking the court to dismiss the action for failing to state a cause of action upon which relief can be granted—in other words, claiming that the plaintiff has not pled a prima facie case. A motion to dismiss tests the sufficiency of the allegations pled in the complaint and may be granted if either the facts do not establish a violation of the law or the law does not provide any relief to the plaintiff.

Motion for Summary Judgment

Either party may file a motion for summary judgment under FRCP 56, asserting that there are no material facts in dispute that rise to a sufficient level to warrant a trial, and that therefore the party is entitled to judgment as a matter of law. Material fact means that the fact is a fact of some consequence to the lawsuit. As an example, if the papers filed by the plaintiff and defendant show that the defendant was speeding and caused the accident in which the plaintiff's car was destroyed, and the parties agree that the car was worth $5,000, then there are no material facts in dispute: the plaintiff should recover $5,000.

When there are no material facts in dispute that rise to such a level, the judge determines how the law resolves this case; a jury does not need to be impaneled. A motion for summary judgment examines the pleadings taken as a whole, as well as all information the parties submit to the court by affidavit in order to determine if there are any factual disputes.

Motions for Judgment as a Matter of Law

Under FRCP Rule 50, motions for judgment as a matter of law test the sufficiency of the proof introduced at trial. The moving party here claims that on the basis of the evidence presented, no reasonable jury could find for the other party. Motions may be requested both pre- and post-verdict. In many state courts, these motions are called motions for directed verdict if filed before the verdict, or motions for judgment notwithstanding the verdict, also known as JNOV, if filed after. The judge must determine if a reasonable jury could find for the plaintiff or defendant, depending on which side moves for the judgment as a matter of law. In addition, through the use of this rule, the judge may increase the jury's verdict (called additur) or reduce it (called remittitur). Motions for judgment as a matter of law test all of the evidence submitted to determine if a reasonable jury could rule in favor of the party opposing the motion.

CIVIL REMEDIES

In a civil case, the plaintiff has the burden of proof—this means the plaintiff must prove her case on both liability and damages. Generally, in a civil case the standard of proof—the extent to which the plaintiff must prove her case—is by a preponderance of the evidence, requiring the plaintiff to tip the scales ever so slightly in her favor. You can think of it this way: in order to get a favorable jury verdict, the plaintiff must simply prove that *more likely than not* (or 51 percent), the plaintiff's allegations are true.

Some civil claims, such as malice, require proof by clear and convincing evidence, which means that the party with the burden of proof must prove to the judge or jury that something is substantially more likely than not to be true. This is the higher standard of proof used in civil cases.

The plaintiff may ask the court for several types of civil remedies. Damages, which are monetary awards, are designed to make the plaintiff whole—to put the plaintiff in the position she would have been but for the defendant's actions. Some damages are designed to compensate the plaintiff for her financial and other non-pecuniary losses.

General damages are non-out-of-pocket costs: they can be hard to quantify and must be calculated by the finder of fact—judge or jury—and they include pain and suffering or loss of enjoyment from an activity that the plaintiff can no longer enjoy. Special damages, on the other hand, are more readily quantifiable—some examples include medical bills or lost wages. In addition, punitive damages may be awarded in rare cases to punish the defendant for wrongful behavior and to deter other people from similar actions in the future.

In some cases, though, money damages will not be enough to make the plaintiff whole. Suppose, for example, that your neighbor began to blare music out of his house in the middle of the night, every night. If you brought suit against your neighbor, you would not only ask for damages, as no amount of money would resolve your dissatisfaction—instead, you would file for an injunction and ask the court to prevent your neighbor from continuing to blare his music.

There are three types of injunctions:

- Temporary restraining orders, which can be granted by the court at the start of the case. Under extraordinary circumstances, ex parte temporary restraining orders, which are issued without notice to the other side, may be obtained.

- Preliminary injunctions, which may be issued after an initial hearing where both parties have the opportunity to present information.

- Permanent injunctions, which are issued only after a full hearing on the merits of the case and remain in force unless reversed on appeal.

Injunctions are one form of equitable remedies, which are nonmonetary remedies that are only granted by a judge, without the need for a jury. Injunctions can be either prohibitory, which prohibit various actions of a party, or mandatory, which force a party to do something. When analyzing whether an injunction should be granted, the court looks at the following five factors:[2]

(1) whether there is an adequate remedy at law (meaning whether money damages would be sufficient to make the plaintiff whole);

(2) whether the plaintiff is likely to succeed on the merits of the case;

(3) whether there is an immediate and irreparable injury being suffered;

(4) whether the balance of the harms tip in favor of granting the injunction; and

(5) whether public policy considerations favor granting the injunction.

Other common forms of equitable remedies include specific performance, where the court compels a party's compliance with a written contract or reformation of the parties' contract; and declaratory relief, where the court determines the legal rights and obligations of the parties.

---

2. *See e.g.*, American Hospital Supply Corp. v. Hospital Products, Ltd., 780 F.2d 589, 593 (7th Cir. 1985).

THE AMERICAN JUDICIAL SYSTEM AND THE APPELLATE PROCESS

In federal and state courts alike, there are different courts that address controversies depending on the stage of the case. Cases begin at the trial-level courts, which have original jurisdiction: this means they can hear new cases and apply the law to the facts in those cases to resolve legal issues. Some trial courts, such as a state district court, can hear most types of controversies; others are limited in the kinds of cases they can decide—a state land court, for example, can only hear cases dealing with that subject. Typically, the jury decides issues of fact—such as whether the light was green or red at the time the defendant drove through it—while the judge decides issues of law, such as whether a motion should be granted or particular evidence should be received by the jury regarding the color of the light. But remember: if a party does not make a jury demand, the judge will decide both issues of fact and law.

A trial court's decision can be appealed. Appellate courts have the power of judicial review: they can review the trial court's decisions for errors and legal mistakes. However, appellate courts do not generally re-examine factual issues, so the facts decided at trial remain the same on appeal.

The federal court system consists of three tiers:

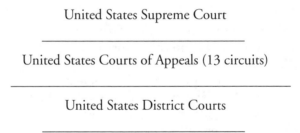

United States Supreme Court

United States Courts of Appeals (13 circuits)

United States District Courts

The appellant, or petitioner, is the party that initiates the appeal; the party answering the appeal is called the appellee, or respondent. While trial court decisions can generally be appealed as a matter of right as long as the appellant has a legal issue or claim, some courts of the highest jurisdiction can refuse to hear cases of their choosing. To get to the United States Supreme Court, for example, a party must file a writ of certiorari—a petition for a case to be reviewed by the Court. The Court may deny the writ and refuse to hear the case, which will make the appellate court decision final. Most state courts follow a three-tiered model that is similar to federal courts, although some states have a two-tiered court system, with their appellate courts acting as the courts of highest jurisdiction. The United States Supreme Court also has the power to review state court decisions.

While appeals make their way up the court system in your jurisdiction, binding authority, as you read previously, makes its way down: in order for a case to have binding authority, it has to come from a higher court in the same jurisdiction.

Q: What are the keys to success as a litigation paralegal?

A: Answer by Gary Melhuish, Manager of Litigation Support Services, Ballard Spahr Andrews & Ingersoll, LLP and Past President of the International Paralegal Management Association:

Attention to detail; frequent communication with supervising attorneys; flexibility; staying on top of current events in litigation; [being a] team player . . . . Making sure that all of the materials required in trial are accessible, organized and in the appropriate presentation format; keeping an eye on the big picture during the trial proceedings to be able to point out trends and events that the lawyers may miss since they are focused on their particular role.

A: Answer by Julie D. Hunt, Litigation Paralegal at Saladino, Oakes & Schaaf, PLLC in Paducah, Kentucky and the 2006 American Association for Justice Paralegal of the Year:

It's the ability to row with the flow: being able to adapt quickly to changing circumstances . . . . Anticipate what's needed. Learn the attorneys' work habits and either work with those habits if they are good or overcome them if they are not. Over time, you will learn what is needed. Don't wait to be told what to do. Make a list of what you think needs to be done and discuss it with the attorney, and if you are in agreement, just make it happen. I have found that the attorney has a lot on his\her plate in preparing for trial. He or she needs to be able to count on you to do certain tasks automatically. Which tasks depends on each paralegal's working relationship with the litigator. I know that I am to automatically: prepare the trial file, set up the war room, draft the pretrial documents, make sure exhibits are complete, line up the witnesses, double-check discovery production, arrange for necessary equipment, prepare subpoenas, ensure travel arrangements are made if necessary, and make sure necessary staff are available and prepared . . . . Whatever it takes to make it happen!

TABLE 1.1: PERSPECTIVES FOR THE ATTORNEY-PARALEGAL TEAM

While your attorney is working on	You might assist by . . . .
• Ensuring that the claim is supported both factually and legally before filing	• Assembling and organizing all the initial supporting documentation for liability and damages
• Deciding on the forum in which to file the case	• Researching federal and state statutes as directed • Researching long-arm statutes and the rules on subject matter jurisdiction, personal jurisdiction, service of process, and venue in your local rules of civil procedure
• Researching additional claims and defenses	• Determining whether there is adequate factual support for those claims and defenses • Determining what documents support your client's claims and defenses • Interviewing the client and witnesses to determine whether the client's claims are supported
• Establishing the fee arrangement between the attorney and client	• Drafting a budget for expected costs and helping the attorney make cost assessments
• Establishing the attorney-client relationship and undertaking representation	• Setting up hard copy and electronic files • Creating an initial database for new matter information • Setting up a "tickler system" to automatically trigger file reviews as necessary

KEY TERMS	
affirmative defense	mediation
answer	minitrial
appeal	motion
appellate court	motion for summary judgment
alternative dispute resolution	motion to dismiss
arbitration	personal jurisdiction
binding authority	plaintiff
collaborative practice	pleadings
conciliation	requests for admissions
Constitution	requests for production
complaint	requests for mental or physical examination
counterclaim	
cross-claim	sanctions
damages	service of process
defendant	settlement
deposition	special damages
discovery	subject matter jurisdiction
early neutral evaluation	summary judgment
injunction	trial court
interrogatories	United States Supreme Court
jurisdiction	venue
legal authority	writ of certiorari
litigation	

DISCUSSION QUESTIONS

1. Your firm is contacted by a new client who was involved in a car accident and suffered serious injuries.

   a. What information would you seek from the client during the initial client interview?

   b. What documents would you ask the client to provide to you?

   c. What jurisdictional factors would you consider before deciding where to file suit?

   d. What are some examples of damages that you would seek on your client's behalf?

   e. What pleadings might be filed by the parties in this case?

2. You represent a corporate defendant from California in a high-volume and complex business dispute in federal court in Massachusetts. The plaintiff accuses the defendant of engaging in various unfair business practices and violations of Massachusetts state law.

   a. What procedural defenses might be available to you?

   b. In attempting to get information from the other side, what discovery methods would you use?

   c. What are some tasks related to discovery that you may assist your attorney with?

   d. What methods of ADR might you discuss with your attorney?

EVIDENCE OVERVIEW

This chapter briefly explains the relevant rules that govern the introduction, exclusion, and admissibility of evidence in court.

CHAPTER OVERVIEW

By the end of this chapter, you should be familiar with

- the concept of relevance;

- rules on witness competency, witness examination, expert witnesses, and impeachment;

- rules on exhibits, real evidence, writings, and demonstrative evidence;

- the concept of privilege;

- the hearsay rule and its many exceptions;

- the paralegal's role in obtaining and safekeeping evidence.

The court admits evidence in order for that information to become part of the jury's consideration and record that is used in deciding a case. The jury cannot consider information that is not formally received into evidence during the trial. Generally, evidence is offered through witnesses testifying on the stand (testimonial evidence) or through the receipt of properly authenticated documents that become part of the record (tangible evidence).

In federal court, evidence must be offered in accordance with the Federal Rules of Evidence, while each state's evidence rules will apply in state courts. While the rules of evidence are complex, it is essential to understand some basic rules of evidence to properly assist your attorney. Let's take a look at five basic rules and some related concepts.

RELEVANCE

Only relevant evidence should be received by the court hearing the matter in dispute: relevant evidence is admissible, while irrelevant evidence is generally inadmissible. The judge will determine which evidence is relevant evidence because the judge determines the admissibility of all evidence. While the judge determines the admissibility of the evidence, the weight of the evidence is left up to the jury. Evidence must also be material: it must concern a fact of consequence to the lawsuit.

Relevance is determined using Rules 401 and 402 of the Federal Rules of Evidence (FRE). Relevant evidence is information that makes a fact of consequence more probable with it than it would be without the information. Think about it this way: in a divorce action, it is generally material to the dissolution of that marriage if the husband beat his wife. But what types of relevant evidence can be used to prove that fact? Relevant evidence could certainly come from someone who saw him strike her. On the other hand, evidence that as a young man the husband frequently engaged in brawls would be irrelevant to the issue of whether he beat his wife. Likewise, suppose that the same man were suing someone for nonpayment of a loan. It would be immaterial to that contract action that the man beat his wife, and therefore that evidence would not be admissible, even if we still had an eyewitness who could offer the evidence.

RULES REGARDING TESTIMONIAL EVIDENCE AND WITNESSES

Competency

Evidence must come from a competent source and generally be known to the witness through personal knowledge. Competency is defined under FRE 601 and 602. While the rules presume that every witness is competent, you must ensure that the witness has the ability to perceive, understand, remember, and communicate the information. You must also ensure that the witness has firsthand knowledge of the matters to which the witness is testifying. Generally, for example, if a witness did not see the car crash, that witness could not testify to how the crash happened; if the witness couldn't remember what happened, she could not testify to what she thinks happened.

Sometimes, witnesses have special issues in regard to competency, such as infancy or insanity, which impair their understanding of the event, so their ability to perceive, understand, remember, and communicate has to be carefully examined. At other times, there may be certain statutory or common-law privileges that exist that will preclude the witnesses' testimony.

Privilege

Privilege addresses a party's right to refuse to testify, prevent another from testifying, or otherwise disclose information. The law of privilege presumes that the relationship between the parties is more important to society in general than the receipt of the information on the specific case in issue. Consider, for example, that the law recognizes the importance of a client being able to tell his lawyer confidential information without fear of that information being disclosed to the court.

Always research and consider if any privileges might preclude testimony by the witness; this includes the attorney-client, priest-penitent, doctor-patient, marital, or other statutory privileges.

Foundation

A proper foundation must be offered before any evidence is received by the court. This means establishing that the information is sufficiently trustworthy to admit into evidence. FRE 901, 902, and 903 provide the information relevant to establishing a proper foundation. As an example, the proper foundation for introduction of the plaintiff's hospital bill can be the hospital's record keeper testifying that this is the plaintiff's bill listing the hospital's actual charges to the plaintiff.

Lay witnesses can testify to information that they have personal knowledge of once the foundation for their knowledge is established. With few exceptions, lay witnesses may only testify to what they have firsthand knowledge of. For example, a lay witness who saw the car crash can tell us what she observed about the car crash, but she cannot testify to what the drivers drank at lunch if she did not observe it.

An expert witness, on the other hand, provides opinion testimony based on his scientific or technical knowledge. For a witness to give opinion testimony, the judge must determine that a foundation has been established showing that the person has some special knowledge or skill that will aid the jury's understanding of the event in question. In the above example, an expert witness can provide his opinion as to what caused the cars to collide once the foundation has been laid that the expert witness has sufficient education, training, background, and experience to offer his opinion testimony. Your attorney will qualify the expert witness at trial by asking questions about the witness's education, training, experience, and background.

To establish the foundation to admit a photograph, someone must testify from personal knowledge what the photograph depicts. For example, the proper foundation for the introduction of a picture taken at the scene of an automobile collision would be a witness who personally saw the scene of the collision and can tell the court that the photo actually portrays the scene. Also keep in mind that there are other issues that may affect the ability to have relevant evidence received, such as chain of custody concerns or the best evidence rule, which deals with proving the contents of a writing, recording, photograph, or other document, and states that the party attempting to prove those contents must offer the original writing, recording, or photograph, or else satisfactorily account for the original's absence.

HEARSAY

There are a host of rules dealing with issues of hearsay. This is an often-confused subject that judges and lawyers struggle with mightily. As a general matter, the rules of hearsay are invoked when a witness on the stand wants to tell the court what she heard instead of what she experienced. If you have ever played the "telephone game" or heard a rumor that was bent and twisted as it was retold, then you should understand why the rules favor receiving information in court from firsthand sources, while disfavoring retelling out-of-court statements. In court, we look for information that is straight from the horse's mouth. Sworn testimony that is based on personal observations and subject to cross-examination is more likely to be a closer version of the truth.

The hearsay rule is invoked when anyone attempts to offer any out-of-court statement to prove the truth of the matter asserted in that statement. When a witness is on the stand and says, "he said," "she said," or even "I said," a hearsay analysis is required. In federal court the hearsay analysis is conducted using FRE 801, 803, 804, and 805.

Hearsay is

1. any statement;

2. made by anyone;

3. anywhere other than while testifying now in this proceeding;

4. if it is offered to prove the truth of the matter asserted in the statement.

For example, suppose that Darius is on trial for murdering Wendy. If Mary testifies that "Allen said that Darius shot Wendy," that is hearsay. Mary is testifying (1) to a statement (2) made by Allen (3) somewhere other than while testifying now in this proceeding (4) and the statement is being offered to prove the matter asserted in the statement—that Darius shot Wendy.

A statement is not hearsay if

- it is not offered to prove the truth of the matter asserted in the statement, but rather offered to prove something else—such as notice or awareness of a certain issue; or

- it is the party's own statement that the other side seeks to offer. For example, if in the case above Mary is called as a witness and testifies that "Darius told me he shot Wendy," then the statement is not hearsay because Darius is a party to the case; it is considered an admission.

Remember that only people make hearsay statements: what you see on a clock or speedometer will not constitute a hearsay statement, nor will a tracking dog pointing to a suspect.

HEARSAY EXCEPTIONS

There are many exclusions and exceptions to the hearsay rule. Under FRE 801, the following are not considered hearsay:

- an agent's statement made while employed by the defendant;

- a coconspirator's statement made in the course or furtherance of the conspiracy;

- the prior statements of a witness who testifies at trial, if the prior statements identify someone; or if the prior statements were inconsistent, and the prior statement was made under oath in a proceeding.

In addition, you should be aware that prior consistent statements of a witness testifying at the present trial can be offered to rebut an express or implied charge of recent fabrication, contrivance, improper influence, or motive.

Hearsay exceptions that permit the receipt of the out-of-court statement because they are deemed sufficiently trustworthy generally fall into three main groups: unavailability exceptions, spontaneous exceptions, and various record exceptions.

Unavailability Exceptions

In order to use what are known as the unavailability exceptions to the hearsay rule, the original speaker of the statement—the declarant—must be unavailable to testify at trial. In order to be considered unavailable under the law, the declarant must be either dead, exercising a privilege, beyond the court's subpoena power, or incompetent. If any one of those conditions is satisfied, then one of the five unavailability exceptions may be used.

The five unavailability exceptions are

- Dying declarations—statements the deceased person made while believing that death was imminent, such as, "Oh Lord, Ursula shot me!"

- Declarations against penal or pecuniary interest—statements against the declarant's then existing penal (think jail time or punishment) or pecuniary (think financial) interests. One example would be, "Peter and I shot Mike."

- Former testimony of a witness—testimony given under oath and subject to cross-examination; for example, testimony by the victim at the arraignment that the defendant hit the victim.

- A statement concerning family history—a statement that reflects records of birth, death, or marriage. One example is, "My mom and dad said I was born on June 25."

- A statement to which you have forfeited your right to object by encouraging the flight of that witness—through the parties' actions, the witness has become unavailable and therefore the witness's earlier statements are now admissible. Bill's statement that "I saw Ursula kill Mike" is admissible if Ursula, through bribery or intimidation, has caused Bill to flee.

Spontaneous Exceptions

There are also spontaneous exceptions to the hearsay rule:

- Present physical condition—a statement that describes the declarant's then existing physical condition. One example is the plaintiff telling his friend Ahmed that "my back still hurts."

- Present mental state—a statement describing the declarant's then existing mental state. A statement by a murder victim to a friend that "I'm going to file for a divorce next week" is admissible as a statement of the murder victim's then existing mental state.

- Statement for the purpose of treatment or diagnosis—a statement made to a health care provider for the purpose of diagnosis or treatment. Plaintiff telling his doctor, "Can you help me, doctor, my back is very sore from a car accident?" is admissible under this exception.

- Excited utterance—sometimes called spontaneous declaration, this is a statement describing or explaining an event or condition, made while under the stress of the event or condition. The statement "Oh God, why did she run that red light and hit my car like this?" may fall into the excited utterance exception.

- Present sense impression—a statement describing an event or condition made while perceiving the event or condition or immediately afterwards. For example, a bystander who yells out, "Look at that car! He's driving so fast, he's going to hurt someone!" just before the car crash has made a present sense impression statement.

Records Exceptions

There are also commonly used records exceptions. Those exceptions and their corresponding FRE sections are

- Business records, Rule 803(6)—records of regularly conducted activities, made by someone with personal knowledge, if kept in the ordinary course of business.

- Public records, Rule 803(8)—records, reports, statements, or data compilations of public offices or agencies as to matters that there was a duty to report.

- Past recollection recorded, Rule 803(5)—a memorandum or record about which a witness had personal knowledge but no longer remembers; some likely examples include diary or journal entries. Past recollection recorded is the only hearsay exception that requires the declarant's presence on the stand in order to provide the required foundation.

- Records of vital statistics, Rule 803(9)—public records or data compilations of births, deaths, or marriage, such as birth or marriage certificates.

- Market reports and commercial lists, Rule 803(17)—these are market reports or commercial lists relied on by the public or persons in particular occupations: for example, a listing of home sales used by brokers, real estate agents, and even homeowners to determine the value of a home.

EXCLUSION OF RELEVANT EVIDENCE UNDER RULE 403

As a final consideration, FRE 403 allows the judge to exclude from the jury's consideration relevant evidence on the grounds of prejudice, confusion, or waste of time. The court has discretion to exclude what would otherwise be admissible evidence if the probative value of the evidence is substantially outweighed by the danger of unfair prejudice, confusion, or delay. This can occur with gruesome photographs, overly sympathetic testimony that has marginal relevance, or simply too many witnesses providing the same testimony. In addition, some evidence is kept out for public policy reasons. Because we do not want to discourage litigants from discussing settlement, or taking remedial measures—such as fixing a broken railing after the plaintiff slipped on the stairs—or offering to pay for medical costs, evidence of these is excluded for relevance and policy reasons.

THE PROCESS AND SCOPE OF WITNESS EXAMINATION AT TRIAL

The central principle of witness examination is preparation, preparation, and more preparation. Proper preparation is needed for both direct examination (where the witness is questioned by the attorney who called him) and cross-examination (where the witness is questioned by the opposing attorney). Despite what you see on television, the best lawyers do not make up their questions on their feet. The best lawyers work and rework both direct and cross-examination questions until the questions are precise and the witnesses know what to expect during their direct examinations. None of it is done extemporaneously. The attorney prepares direct and cross-examinations to support the chosen theme of the case with an eye toward reminding the jury of the important evidence at the conclusion of the case when she delivers the summation.

During direct examination the attorney tells her client's story by eliciting information from witnesses. Good direct examinations, like any good story, have an interesting beginning, a good middle, and a great end. Direct examinations should tell us the "who, what, when, where, how, and why" of the story. Questions on direct examination, with few exceptions, must be nonleading questions. A nonleading question, and one that advances a good story, starts with "who, what, where, when, describe, how, or why." On direct examination, the witnesses should look at the jury to make contact and establish a relationship with them as they testify.

Impeachment

The best lawyers view cross-examination as providing an opportunity to present their version of the events through the opponent's witnesses while impeaching the witness on key points where the testimony supports the adversary. Witnesses should never be allowed to ramble in response to a question, and the questions should only be leading questions—questions that must be answered with a simple yes or no. As you help your attorney write questions for witnesses, remember to follow these rules.

Every witness who testifies places his character for truthfulness in question and is therefore subject to cross-examination. The witness may be cross-examined concerning his bias (relationship to a party in the case creates an inference of bias); credibility (prior convictions and untruthful acts raise issues of the witness's credibility); and matters pertaining to the testimony given on direct examination (for example, that the witness was not at the event as claimed, did not see everything he claimed to see, or even has perception difficulties).

Objections

Objections made at trial must be clear and precise. They can be used to keep evidence out and to disrupt examinations and the flow of the opposing side's case. Well-timed objections to protect a witness are one of the important functions of the well-prepared advocate. Attorneys use the specific legal basis that supports the objection when they stand to voice an objection to testimony. For example: "Objection: hearsay, it is an out-of-court statement . . . ." or "Objection: relevance, it does not help prove . . . ."

The responses to objections should be equally clear: "Your Honor, it is not hearsay, as it is not offered to prove the truth of the matter asserted. It is offered to show notice"; or "Your Honor, it is relevant because it goes to the witness's state of mind, which is an issue in this case."

Exhibits, Real Evidence, Writings, and Demonstrative Evidence

When offering physical evidence through a witness, it is important to lay a proper foundation that establishes that the information is reliable and trustworthy. Beyond that, it is important to be courteous and follow some tried and true mechanics in preparing the examinations. To formally offer physical evidence at trial through a witness: ask "Please state your name," and then "Please describe how . . . ."

After providing some more foundation questions that establish the authenticity of the information and competency of the witness, the questions are directed at providing a foundation for the court to receive the document in evidence. The document should be shown to counsel for the adverse party so the attorney can examine it. Make sure your attorney has a courtesy copy for the opposing attorney to review as your attorney has the document marked for identification.

When offering evidence, attorneys often make the following foundation statements or questions:

- May I approach the bench to have a document marked for identification?

- May I approach the witness to have him identify the document?

- May I approach the witness to retrieve the document?

- I now move the document into evidence.

At that point, any objections to the evidence will be heard by the court. Make sure you have researched the issues so that your attorney can properly respond to likely objections to the proposed evidence. On particularly difficult evidentiary issues, it is advisable to have copies of cases supporting the receipt of the evidence. Your attorney can provide this case law to the court to support the judge's ruling. Remember, in trial work as in life, the key is preparation, preparation, and more preparation.

The Paralegal's Role in Obtaining and Safekeeping Documents and Evidence

There are two main roles for the paralegal in this regard. One is to collect and assemble important documents and pretrial evidence in admissible form. The other is coordinating the use of that information with the attorney both during and at trial, depending on the role you will play with the attorney during the trial of the case. While this chapter provided general information about the admissibility of evidence, Part II of this book assists you with collecting, assembling, and coordinating the use of evidence in practice.

TABLE 2.1: PERSPECTIVES FOR THE ATTORNEY-PARALEGAL TEAM

While your attorney is working on	You might assist by . . . .
• Anticipating and planning for evidentiary issues that might arise at trial	• Researching evidentiary rules and finding cases (or one dead-on case) that are exactly on point
• Choosing the "top documents" that he or she wants to introduce at trial	• Helping the attorney select the documents • Assembling documents • Making copies or electronic images of the documents • Organizing the documents • Creating cross-indexes as needed
• Anticipating evidentiary objections by and issues from your opponent	• Researching issues from your opponent's standpoint • Finding legal authority that supports the client's side • Assembling relevant factual support and documents
• Anticipating authentication issues	• Obtaining certified copies where available, documents with official seals, or other proof for self-authentication • Researching evidentiary rules to see under what methods various documents may be admissible
• Anticipating hearsay issues and objections	• Researching hearsay exceptions and any case law • Serving as the attorney's sounding board on hearsay issues and responses

• Weighing the witnesses' competency and credibility	• Re-interviewing witnesses and gathering factual support for witnesses' testimony

KEY TERMS	
competency	impeachment
cross-examination	lay witness
demonstrative evidence	material
direct examination	privilege
evidence	real evidence
exhibits	relevance
expert witness	prejudice, confusion, or undue waste of time
foundation	privilege
hearsay	testimonial evidence
hearsay exceptions	unavailability rule

DISCUSSION QUESTIONS

1. You represent the plaintiff in a negligence suit that resulted from an automobile collision. Which of the following evidence will be admissible at trial? Which evidentiary rule(s) would you need to consult to determine the admissibility of each of these? Who do you think you will need as witnesses in order to offer the evidence? What are the foundational requirements that you have to establish in order to admit each of the following pieces of evidence?

   a. Photographs depicting damages to the plaintiff's car.

   b. A copy of the defendant's birth certificate.

   c. A conversation between the defendant and her husband about the accident, held two hours after the accident in the couple's home.

   d. The defendant's offer to settle the case out of court.

   e. Testimony by a six-year-old bystander who witnessed the accident.

2. In the case above, your attorney is attempting to introduce the following statements in court. Determine whether the statements constitute hearsay; if so, determine whether there are any hearsay exceptions available to you:

a. A statement by the defendant at the accident scene: "I am terribly sorry; I must have dozed off and went right through the red light."

b. A statement by a bystander at the accident scene: "Look out for that car going through the red light!"

c. A statement in the police report: "Witness stated that she observed the driver go through the red light just before impact."

d. The defendant's speed at the time of collision, deduced from 60 feet of skid marks.

e. The defendant's speedometer, broken upon impact, showing that the speed was 65 miles per hour.

3

WHAT TO EXPECT BEFORE AND AT TRIAL

This chapter describes the trial process and explains the paralegal's role in trial preparation and assistance during trial, using a fictitious case to illustrate what happens before and during the trial process.

CHAPTER OVERVIEW

By the end of this chapter, you should be familiar with

- the trial process;

- pretrial procedures;

- opening statements;

- the process of introducing evidence and witness examination at trial;

- jury instructions;

- closing arguments;

- the attorney's involvement through the trial;

- the paralegal's role in assisting the attorney through the trial process.

MEET THE PARTIES

Mimi and Christopher Woodward are siblings. The Woodwards are African-American, which is a protected class under federal civil rights statutes.

One late afternoon, Mimi picked up Christopher from his oral surgeon's office where Christopher had just undergone oral surgery. Christopher's oral surgeon prescribed oxycontin and antibiotics for follow-up care, and a nurse in his office called the prescription in at WelcomeMart, a pharmacy where Christopher was a long-time customer. At the prescriptions counter, a store manager told Christopher he would have to wait a while for his medicine, as they needed to verify insurance information.

Christopher decided to pick up a few items at the store. Mimi soon after entered the store and was accosted by the security guard on duty, who instructed the manager to call out for the police officer on detail in the store. The police officer ran to the aisle with his nightstick out and in an agitated state said to the Woodwards, "You don't belong here, do you?" The officer and security guard then forced the Woodwards into a small enclosed space near the entrance to the store. After putting them in the room, the officer and guard confronted the Woodwards. With his face just inches from Christopher and Mimi, the guard yelled at them, "I know your type, and I know how you people act! I am not going to let you leave until you tell me you took those drugs; then the other police will come and arrest you."

The Woodwards explained that they had taken nothing, but the officers simply laughed at them, and the guard would not let them leave. The guard continued to question the Woodwards, even as the room began to get very hot. Mimi then told the guard and the officer about Christopher's oral surgery, which left Christopher in a great deal of pain. The guard responded, "I don't believe you people. I watch the news! Where do you keep your knives?"

The store manager came into the room and informed the guard and officer that more police were on the way. When the police arrived, they questioned the Woodwards, concluded that nothing had been stolen, and allowed them to leave. Christopher continues to suffer great pain and emotional distress as a result of the incident. He was hospitalized with a serious staph infection and spent ten days in the hospital on intravenous antibiotics. In fact, six months after the incident, Christopher's physician continues to treat him in order to restore his health. Christopher has also missed work and incurred significant medical expenses as a result of the incident at WelcomeMart.

MEET THE PARALEGALS

Patty is a paralegal at Small & Mighty, P.C., a five-attorney firm in the Woodwards' hometown that specializes in representing plaintiffs in personal injury matters. Patty assists both partners with trial preparation, legal research, and fact gathering. The Woodwards seek Patty's firm to represent them in their case against WelcomeMart.

Danny is a paralegal in the Nita City office of Big & Better, LLP, a large national firm. Danny works in the firm's litigation practice group and assists Attorney Better, a partner who handles litigation matters for various corporate clients, including WelcomeMart. Although WelcomeMart has an in-house legal department, its attorneys handle mostly transactional matters such as contract work, licensing, and mergers and acquisitions. WelcomeMart's general counsel outsources litigation matters to various large law firms—and in the Woodwards' case against the corporation, the general counsel calls Danny's firm for help.

Let's follow *Woodward v. WelcomeMart* through the pretrial and trial process—and examine Patty and Danny's respective paralegal tasks as the case unfolds.

INITIAL CLIENT INTERVIEWS

Patty prepares for an initial client interview with the Woodwards. From the short phone call she has conducted with the Woodwards, she has deduced that the Woodwards' case will potentially involve civil rights violations and false imprisonment claims. Patty first checks to make sure that there are no conflicts within the firm in representing the Woodwards. Once satisfied that no conflict exists, there is much to be done. Patty consults a litigation form book for sample interview checklists to use in these types of suits. She also checks her firm's own sample checklists. Finally, she checks with Attorney Mighty about any additional questions to ask during the interview.

Patty welcomes the Woodwards into her office, making sure that the prospective clients are comfortable. She also makes sure to minimize interruptions during the interview. Patty ensures that the interview will comport with ethical rules protecting client confidentiality—for example, she puts away all client files and closes out of computer files that list client information before she takes the Woodwards into her office.

Using her checklist, Patty interviews the Woodwards. She first asks them for personal information and then asks the Woodwards to describe what happened during and after their detention. She asks the Woodwards about the types of relief they would like to seek in the case. When the Woodwards ask Patty for advice about the potential defenses WelcomeMart could claim, Patty explains to them that she is a paralegal and cannot answer their question—as a nonlawyer, Patty cannot provide legal advice, represent another person in court, or establish the attorney-client relationship. Patty tells the Woodwards that they should give her copies of all the documentation they have in the matter, including their doctors' bills, medical records, police reports, and any other information they have that will provide a clearer picture of the issues involved in the case.

After the interview, Patty drafts an intake memorandum to Attorney Mighty describing the interview. In it, she lists the clients' personal information, facts about the case, the relief sought by the client, and the next steps that should be taken in the case. After reviewing Patty's memorandum, Attorney Mighty meets with the Woodwards for a consultation. The Woodwards decide to retain Attorney Mighty to represent them in their suit. They sign a contingency fee agreement, which spells out the scope of representation, the attorney fees to be collected if the plaintiffs are successful, and the types of costs for which the clients will be responsible.

SETTLEMENT ISSUES

Patty next drafts a demand letter to the potential defendants in the Woodwards' case. In it, she briefly describes the Woodwards' claims against the store, the relief they seek, and the date by which they want that relief in order to settle the matter without going to court.

Danny has his first meeting with Attorney Better and the general counsel of WelcomeMart, who has received the plaintiffs' demand letter. Attorney Better discusses settlement options with the client, possible causes of action and defenses, and the next steps to investigate the facts and obtain pertinent documents relating to the plaintiffs' potential claims. The general counsel expresses her preference to keep the case out of court to reduce litigation costs and avoid negative publicity.

Patty and Danny both play an integral role in the settlement process: they ensure that proper documentation and support exists for the claims and defenses and that it is readily available to support the attorneys' arguments on the value of the claim for settlement purposes. They also act as conduit for information between the clients and attorneys.

PLEADINGS

Patty conducts legal and factual research to help Attorney Mighty ensure that the Woodwards' claims have evidentiary support as well as a good-faith legal basis.

Because the Woodwards' claims involve a federal civil rights violation, Attorney Mighty decides to file the case in United States District Court in Nita City, in the district where the incident took place. The court will have the authority to hear both the federal civil rights claim and any state claims under the supplemental jurisdiction doctrine. Patty familiarizes herself with the Federal Rules of Civil Procedure, which will govern the procedural issues in the case.

Using her firm's template or reviewing similar pleadings filed on behalf of other parties, Patty drafts a complaint on the Woodwards' behalf. In it, she includes a caption; a statement of jurisdiction; a statement identifying the parties; the plaintiffs' claims; the damages sought by the plaintiffs; the plaintiffs' demand for a jury trial; and the attorney's subscription, or signature block. Attorney Mighty carefully reviews Patty's draft and notes his changes. After the staff or Patty make the changes he requested, Attorney Mighty signs the complaint and instructs Patty to file the complaint electronically in federal court, in accordance with the local rules of court. The clerk of the court acknowledges receipt and provides Patty with a docket number and summons.

Next, Patty must serve the defendants with process. She attaches a copy of the complaint to the summons, which orders the defendants to answer the allegations asserted by the plaintiff. Patty uses the information she previously obtained from the Secretary of State's website regarding WelcomeMart's state of incorporation, principal place of business, and registered agent to serve the agent on the corporation's behalf. She also serves the proper agent of the City of Nita, another named defendant because of the actions of the police officer who is employed by the city.

WelcomeMart's legal department sends Attorney Better a copy of the Woodwards' complaint. Attorney Better decides to first file a motion to dismiss under FRCP 12(b), alleging that the Woodwards' complaint fails to state a claim upon which relief can be granted—that is, based on existing law, the plaintiffs lack a prima facie case. Danny drafts the motion and a short memorandum of law containing the case authority that supports the request to dismiss the case. This is carefully reviewed and signed by Attorney Better. Danny then files the motion and memorandum with the court in which the Woodwards filed their case. He serves a copy of the motion on Attorney Mighty. Patty and her attorney then prepare their response to the motion and file a memorandum of law detailing why the case should not be dismissed.

Shortly thereafter, the trial judge weighs the arguments and denies the defendant's motion to dismiss. WelcomeMart now has ten days to file its answer to the Woodwards' complaint. Danny dockets the deadline, carefully noting it on the firm's master calendar as well as Attorney Better's individual calendar.

Danny is entrusted with interviewing the WelcomeMart employees who were working at the time of the incident and reviewing any security tapes that exist. He gathers other factual information and performs legal research about potential affirmative defenses on WelcomeMart's behalf. Danny then drafts the defendant's answer, denying the plaintiff's allegations that are untrue. Danny adds an affirmative defense saying that WelcomeMart employees were authorized by law to detain the Woodwards to investigate the possibility that the Woodwards were shoplifting. Attorney Better reads and signs the answer, and Danny files it with the court, then serves a copy on the plaintiffs' attorney.

DISCOVERY

After the exchange of the initial disclosure information required by the FRCP, discovery comes next. Attorney Mighty decides to depose Bart Harayda, the WelcomeMart security guard who was on duty at the time of the incident. Patty sends out a deposition notice and a subpoena to the security guard. She then dockets the deposition's date and also schedules a transcriptionist to attend the deposition and take down the record. The attorneys and parties will attend the deposition. Whether the paralegals attend the deposition or not, they will assist in getting the attorney ready for this important discovery tool. Patty helps Attorney Mighty prepare his questions for the deponent. Patty consults a litigation form book for sample deposition questions and carefully reviews all the documentary evidence for additional areas of inquiry.

The following is an excerpt from Bart Harayda's deposition:

DEPOSITION OF BART HARAYDA

Witness was first sworn by the stenographer. Plaintiffs' attorney conducts the examination.

Q. Please state your name and spell your last name.

A. My name is Bart Harayda, H-A-R-A-Y-D-A.

Q. Where do you live?

A. Right here at 131 Center Street in Nita City.

Q. Where do you work?

A. I am the security guard in town at WelcomeMart, the drug super-store.

Q. How long have you been so employed?

A. Almost eighteen months now.

Q. Where did you previously work?

A. I didn't, I was attending Nita High.

Q. What training did you receive from WelcomeMart since they hired you?

A. On my first day there, they showed me around, gave me my uniform, and said to watch out for the kids and druggies, as they were always trying to rip us off.

Q. What specific training did you receive regarding detaining or arresting shoplifters?

A. Nothing special. Just watch out for them and hold them until the police come. They won't give me a gun.

* * *

Q. At some point, you claim you received a security advisory regarding suspected drug thieves, right?

A. Yes, we get security advisories all the time from headquarters. They really are concerned about losing money.

Q. And that advisory told you to be on watch for African-Americans wearing hooded sweatshirts, right?

A. Yes.

Q. Did the advisory describe the suspects?

A. Yeah, they were black and wearing hooded sweatshirts.

Q. Was there any other description beyond what you just described?

A. No, just what I said.

Q. Did it describe the suspects' height?

A. No.

Q. Did it describe their weight?

A. No, I told you what it said.

Q. Did it describe the suspects as light or dark skinned?

A. No.

Q. Did it describe the length or color of their hair?

A. No.

Q. Did the alert include any physical descriptions about the suspects?

A. They were black, in hooded sweatshirts, and stealing drugs.

* * *

Q. What happened on the day you first saw Mimi and Christopher Woodward in the Welcomemart?

A. I went into action. I saw a car right in front of the store with its engine running. I saw Christopher Woodward walk away from the counter and grab something off the shelf. Then he went into his backpack as the other one came down the aisle. I knew this was it.

Q. What do you mean by you "knew this was it"?

A. They were the suspects. Both were black. Both wore hooded sweatshirts even though one of them didn't have the hood up. She was black.

Q. What did you do then?

A. I called for Officer Brayton, the city detail officer, and we approached them and quickly grabbed them before they could run.

Q. Why did you grab them?

A. They were the drug thieves.

Q. What had they done in the store at that point?

A. It looked like Christopher took something, and he was a match.

Q. What specifically did you see Christopher Woodward take?

A. I couldn't be sure, but it was clear he was up to no good.

Q. What happened next?

A. We told them we needed to speak with them and asked them to come with us to the office.

Q. Did they protest?

A. A little at first; they got mouthy, but eventually quieted down and came along. We didn't have to hit them or anything.

Q. What happened next?

A. We took them to the office.

Q. Did you close the door?

A. Yes, that's procedure.

Q. Where did you learn that procedure?

A. I don't know. I just learned it.

Q. Did you lock the door?

A. Yes, I'm supposed to.

Q. Why do you say you're supposed to?

A. Well, if the door is not locked, they could get out easier.

* * *

Q. Did they say anything to you or officer Brayton during the time in Welcomemart's office?

A. Yes, they said something about them being sick, but they all say something to try and get out of the office.

Q. What happened when the police came?

A. They asked them questions, searched them, and then let them go.

Q. And the police searched them in front of you, didn't they?

A. Yes, they did.

Q. And the police found no stolen property on either of the Wood-wards, did they?

A. No.

Meanwhile, Danny prepares the defendant's first set of interrogatories to the Woodwards. In it, he asks clear questions about the Woodwards' recollection of the incident, as well as requests for personal information. After Attorney Better reviews the interrogatories, Danny serves them on Attorney Mighty. Patty reviews the interrogatories for objections and drafts a cover letter instructing the Woodwards that they must draft a response to each interrogatory within thirty days and forwards the interrogatories to the clients.

Patty's firm drafts a request for the production of documents to WelcomeMart. Patty also receives the transcript of the security guard's deposition, a document that's well over 300 pages long. She's entrusted with digesting the deposition: she summarizes the document with specific page and line notations of important points.

SUMMARY JUDGMENT

Both parties file for a motion for summary judgment under FRCP 56, claiming that there are no issues of material fact that rise to a "triable" level, and that as a matter of law, the judge should rule for their client. Patty and Danny assist their attorneys with preparing the motion, which consists of the motion itself, a legal memorandum, and accompanying affidavits. Danny performs legal research and helps draft Attorney Better's memorandum of law. Patty, meanwhile, helps draft affidavits by the Woodwards detailing their recollection of the facts surrounding the incident. After taking the motions under advisement, the judge denies both parties' motions for summary judgment, and the case proceeds to a final pretrial conference in anticipation of a trial shortly thereafter.

PRETRIAL CONFERENCE

Patty and Danny review all essential information with their attorneys well before the final pretrial conference. They each discuss with their attorneys what specifically the attorneys want Patty and Danny to prepare, and what additional information the attorneys need to have a successful final pretrial conference.

Attorney Mighty and Attorney Better meet for a pretrial conference, where they discuss the possibility of settlement, simplifying the issues, and stipulating to facts that are not in dispute. They also identify the witnesses, including Christopher Woodward, his treating physician, and the security guard on duty at the time of the incident. Attorney Mighty and Attorney Better also pre-number the exhibits they plan to introduce at trial—for example, a copy of Christopher's prescription.

VOIR DIRE

Next comes the jury selection process. Potential jurors gather in the jury pool room after being summonsed to court to serve on a jury. The judge first reviews the questionnaires the potential jurors have completed with the attorneys and excuses any jurors who are not qualified to serve or for whom there would be extreme hardship to serve as a juror.

Often the attorneys for both sides question the potential jurors. In some jurisdictions, only the judge will ask the jurors questions. Patty and Danny both assist their attorneys with putting together their juror questionnaires, using sample questionnaires from prior cases and form books.

Each attorney gets to challenge jurors. There are challenges for cause, where the attorneys must give a reason for not wanting a particular juror to serve on the jury—for example, Attorney Mighty challenges one juror for cause on the basis of bias because the juror is a former WelcomeMart employee. There are also a limited number of peremptory challenges for each attorney. Here, the attorneys do not have to give a reason for challenging a juror. After both attorneys go through their challenges, the jurors and any alternates are impaneled.

OPENING STATEMENTS

Opening statements begin the trial. Attorney Mighty goes first; his clients have the burden of proving their case by a preponderance of the evidence. Attorney Mighty recounts the important facts of the case to the jury, explaining that the facts will show a violation of the Woodwards' rights:

> Good afternoon, your Honor. My name is Peter Mighty, and it is my honor to deliver the opening statement for Christopher and Mimi Woodward, the plaintiffs.
>
> There was once a dream that we would be judged not by what we looked like or where we came from, but by the content of our character. The testimony will show that on June 11, when Christopher and Mimi Woodward entered the WelcomeMart store, they were judged not by the content of their character, but instead were targeted by the head of security at that store, Bart Harayda, and Officer Brayton of Nita City simply because they were African-American.
>
> The Woodwards were profiled, pressured, and put in pain. The testimony will show that the defendant WelcomeMart's employees, Harayda, the head of security, and Shadique Grayson, the store manager, as well as Officer Brayton of Nita City, profiled the Woodwards because of what they looked like and what they wore. They then pressured and pushed them into a tiny, hot,

closed room to coerce them to confess to something they never did. The pain the plaintiffs suffered that day from prejudice marks us all.

* * *

The Woodwards will testify today to going to the WelcomeMart to have Christopher's pain medication filled, as he had just had oral surgery. When Christopher went to the prescription counter, the testimony of plaintiffs' and defendant's witnesses will show that he was falsely told that the insurance needed to be verified and he would have to wait. At that point, Harayda sprang into action to send a message. He did so because he and the store manager had concocted a plan to profile any African-American person who came into the store in a hooded sweatshirt as a shoplifter.

While Christopher was waiting for the computers to verify insurance, his concerned sister came to look for him. Harayda then grabbed the Woodwards and pushed them into that tiny, hot, confined space while threatening them to force them to confess to something they never did. Profiled, pressured, and with the pain mounting, Christopher's surgery was now taking its toll, and Mimi's diabetic condition grew steadily worse.

In that tiny, hot, closed room, Harayda screamed. "I know you people," he threatened. "I am not going to let you leave until you tell me you took the drugs. I will call the police and have you arrested." Profiled, pressured, and put in pain.

* * *

This abuse went on not for five minutes, not ten minutes, not twenty minutes, but more than thirty. Only when the police finally arrived were the Woodwards freed from their confinement in that tiny, hot, closed room. The testimony will prove that any claims that the Woodwards took anything that day are false. Even the defendant's own store manager will testify that the Woodwards stole nothing.

The evidence and testimony today will show by a preponderance of the evidence that

1. The store's employees profiled the Woodwards because they were African-American and dressed in hooded sweatshirts.

2. The Woodwards were pushed around and pressured to confess to something that they simply did not do.

3. Because of their employees' reprehensible actions, WelcomeMart and the City of Nita inflicted horrible pain upon the Woodwards.

* * *

When Christopher and Mimi Woodward walked into WelcomeMart that afternoon, they were not asking anyone to like or dislike them. All they asked was to be judged by their character; instead, they were treated with disrespect. Harayda wanted to send a message to African-American people, and he did. The testimony we will offer today will show what happens when prejudice, profiling, and pressure are allowed to go unchecked. At the conclusion of all the testimony here today, we will ask you to find WelcomeMart and the City of Nita liable for civil rights violations and the false imprisonment of Christopher and Mimi Woodward.

Thank you.

Attorney Better then makes his opening statement on behalf of WelcomeMart:

Good morning. My name is Joseph Better, and I represent Mr. Shadique Brown and Mr. Bart Harayda of the defendant, WelcomeMart.

First, let's remember that every story has both good and bad parts—and there are always, always two sides to every story.

Let's first discuss the good. Mr. Brown and Ms. Harayda will testify here today as to their good faith, their good intentions to prevent shoplifters so they can keep prices low and serve their community, and their good treatment of the plaintiffs while they asked them about their unusual behavior that day—such as the car running right outside the pharmacy door, the angry confrontation between the Woodwards in the store, and one plaintiff reaching into the bag in an aisle.

* * *

The testimony will show that a series of drug thefts had occurred in the surrounding area. Concerned, my client WelcomeMart tried to be on watch for suspicious activity.

You will hear testimony from Bart Harayda, the head of security at WelcomeMart, who will tell you that he received a security advisory. He will also describe the plaintiffs' unusual behavior in the store that day. Bart Harayda is experienced and successful at catching shoplifters.

Shadique Brown, the store manager, will also describe the plaintiffs' unusual behavior in the store that day. Testimony will show that the Woodwards wore hooded sweatshirts and sunglasses, just like drug thieves who had visited WelcomeMart in the past, and whom they were told to be looking out for. The testimony will show that one plaintiff initially stayed in the car.

Fearing suspicious behavior, Bart will tell you that he politely asked the Woodwards to come to his office to talk to him. They agreed; who wouldn't? More good faith and good intentions. The testimony will show that the Woodwards voluntarily went into the office. After they chatted, the police came and talked to them, and everyone left and went about their business.

* * *

At the end of the case, after you have heard not just the plaintiffs' evidence but the defendants' as well—and please keep an open mind until then—we will ask you to return a verdict for the defendant WelcomeMart.

WITNESS EXAMINATION

Next the parties introduce evidence—both tangible evidence and testimonial evidence offered through witnesses. First, Attorney Mighty conducts a direct examination of the plaintiffs' witnesses, who are then cross-examined by Attorney Better.

The direct examination of Christopher Woodward takes place as follows:

Attorney Mighty: Good Morning, Mr. Woodward. Please state your name.

Woodward: Christopher Woodward.

M: What is your national origin?

W: African-American.

* * *

M: Turning your attention to June 11, what did you do around 9:00 a.m. that morning?

W: I had a doctor's appointment to undergo oral surgery, so my sister Mimi gave me a ride to the oral surgeon's office.

M: Why did you not drive yourself to the oral surgeon's office?

W: I was going to have anesthesia and needed a ride.

M: What happened immediately after your surgery?

W: I had to pick up the prescription for pain pills, for the pain from the surgery at WelcomeMart.

M: How was it that the prescription was at WelcomeMart?

W: The nurse at the oral surgeon's office sent it over to them.

M: Why was it sent over to WelcomeMart?

W: It was done so it would be waiting for me when I got to Welcome-Mart.

M: Around what time did your sister Mimi pick you up at the surgeon's office?

W: She picked me up around 1:00 p.m.

M: How did she appear when she picked you up from the surgeon's office?

W: She was pale and a little disheveled. Mimi is diabetic and has to eat on a regular schedule.

M: After your sister picked you up, where did you go?

W: We went to WelcomeMart.

M: What did you do when you got to the WelcomeMart store?

W: I went in alone into the store while Mimi waited outside.

M: What happened when you went into that WelcomeMart?

W: I do not always go to that store, so it took me a minute to find the pharmacist. I went to the counter.

M: What happened at the counter?

W: They told me that they had to verify the insurance.

* * *

M: What happened next?

W: I gave my prescription to the pharmacist and began shopping for a cold drink or ice cream to ease the pain.

M: Where was your sister Mimi at this time?

W: She was waiting in the car.

M: What happened while you were shopping around the store?

W: Mimi came into the store. She began to call my name; she was worried about what was taking so long.

M: What happened while Mimi was talking to you?

W: A security guard came out of nowhere, grabbed Mimi by the arm, and got in our face. The guard called for the cop Brayton to come, and they pushed me into Mimi, pushing the both of us into a tiny room.

M: Do you see that same security guard in the court today?

W: Yes.

M: Can you point him out and describe an article of clothing?

W: (Points at Mr. Harayda.) He is wearing the yellow tie at that table.

M: Please let the record reflect that the witness has identified Bart Harayda. Do you see Officer Brayton in the court today?

W: Yes.

M: Can you point Officer Brayton out and describe an article of clothing?

W: (Points at Officer Brayton.) Officer Brayton is seated at that table and has a badge on his shirt.

M: Please let the record reflect that the witness has identified Officer Brayton. Now can you describe the room in which you were confined?

W: Yes, it was cramped, hot, small, and dimly lit, approximately ten feet by ten feet.

M: What did the guard say to you?

W: He began yelling at us, saying, "I know you took the drugs, I saw you! I know you people! I am not letting you go until you tell me you took the drugs; then I will call the other police and have you arrested."

M: Were you able to leave the room?

W: No; he turned and locked the door and then stood between us and the door.

M: What did he do with you while in the room with him?

W: The guard continued to yell at us. We could not get out, and I wanted the police to come and rescue us from these madmen.

M: How did you feel when you were in the room?

W: Sick, humiliated, worried about them hurting us. It was horrible.

M: May I approach the bench to have a document marked for identification, your Honor? May I approach the witness to have him identify this document?

I now hand you what has been previously marked for identification. Please describe what the document is.

W: It was my prescription information that was attached to the bag when I picked up my medication from WelcomeMart.

M: Your Honor, may I approach the witness to retrieve the document? Your Honor, I now move the item previously marked for identification purpose into evidence. (Document received into evidence and marked as an exhibit.)

M: Why did you not pick up the prescription the first day you were at WelcomeMart?

W: I was too distraught and sick that day. I just could not stay a minute longer; the whole experience was sickening and humiliating.

M: Thank you, Mr. Woodward. No further questions for this witness, your Honor.

Next, Attorney Better stands up to cross-examine the witness:

Attorney Better: You went into the store wearing a hooded sweatshirt, correct?

Woodward: Yes.

B: Your sister waited in the running car just outside the door, right?

W: Yes.

B: Your mouth was sore, correct?

W: Yes.

B: In addition, you were a little groggy from the anesthesia, right?

W: Yes.

B: You walked around the aisles while waiting for your medicine, cor-
    rect?

W: Yes. I was looking for some ice cream and a cold drink.

B: At some point while walking into the store, you reached into your
    bag, right?

W: Yes.

B: Your sister came into the store walking swiftly, right?

W: Yes.

B: She was impatient, was she not?

W: Yes.

B: She yelled for you, correct?

W: Yes.

B: Eventually, the guard and police officer came to talk to the two of
    you, correct?

W: Yes.

B: And you both voluntary went in the office, right?

W: Not really; we . . .

B: Well, you were not carried into the office, right?

W: No.

B: And you were not dragged into the office, right?

W: No.

B: And you never specifically asked to leave, right?

W: No.

B: And you never got up when you were in that room and told them
    you were leaving either, right?

W: No.

* * *

B: No one pointed a gun at you, right?

W: No.

B: No one beat you, right?

W: No.

B: In fact, the truth is, you were polite and you cooperated, right?

W: Yes.

B: And your sister was polite and cooperative as well, was she not?

W: Yes.

B: Prior to this incident, you did not ask your sister to pick up your prescription, right?

W: No.

B: You did not fill your prescription that day, right?

W: No.

B: And you did not fill your prescription the next day either, correct?

W: No.

B: No one physically prevented you from filling your prescription the next day, correct?

W: No.

B: By the way, you eventually got it filled, didn't you?

W: Yes.

B: At a WelcomeMart, too, right?

W: Yes.

B: Your Honor, I have no further questions for this witness. Thank you.

The examination of the plaintiffs' witnesses continues in this manner: Attorney Mighty examines and Attorney Better cross-examines each witness. When Attorney Mighty rests, witnesses for the defense are examined by Attorney Better and then cross-examined by Attorney Mighty.

MOTION FOR JUDGMENT AS A MATTER OF LAW BEFORE THE VERDICT

Before the jury has a chance to deliberate on the evidence presented in the case, Attorney Better files a motion for judgment as a matter of law. He asks the judge to rule for the defendants without giving the case to the jury because no reasonable jury could rule for the plaintiffs based on applicable law and the evidence they submitted during the trial.

Danny had helped Attorney Better prepare the memorandum of law that is filed with the motion. He performed the legal research to find favorable past cases that addressed the same legal and factual issues and assisted with drafting the motion and memorandum.

The judge denies Attorney Better's motion, and the case proceeds to a jury determination.

CLOSING ARGUMENTS

After all the parties' evidence is introduced, the attorneys make their closing arguments to the jury. They focus on arguing their clients' respective cases based on the facts received into evidence and applicable law.

Attorney Better goes first, delivering his closing argument for the defendants:

> Good morning, again my name is Joseph Better. I have been privileged to represent Ms. Shadique Brown and Mr. Bart Harayda of WelcomeMart, a drugstore.
>
> (To the judge.) May I please use the enlarged exhibits to illustrate my closing?
>
> So now you know, as I told you in my opening, that just like in every other story, this story has both good and bad parts—and there are always, always, always two sides to every story. The plaintiffs have not shown by a preponderance of the evidence that they were imprisoned against their will or that their civil rights were violated. This case is simply a matter of bad timing.
>
> * * *
>
> Ms. Brown and Mr. Harayda testified here today to their good faith; their good intentions to prevent shoplifters so they can keep prices low and serve their community; and their good treatment of the plaintiffs while they asked them about their unusual behavior that day. Remember the testimony? The plaintiffs left the car running right outside the door. They then had an angry confrontation

between them while in the store, and Christopher was seen reaching into his bag in the aisle.

The testimony showed that a series of drug thefts had occurred in the surrounding area and an alert was issued. Concerned, my client, WelcomeMart, was on watch for suspicious activity. Bart Harayda, the head of security at WelcomeMart, told you that he received a security advisory. He described the plaintiffs' unusual behavior in the store that day. Bart Harayda is experienced in catching shoplifters and has been successful in the past doing so.

Shadique Brown, the store manager, also described the plaintiffs' unusual behavior in the store that day. Remember the security advisory. Testimony will show that the Woodwards wore hooded sweatshirts and sunglasses, just like the shoplifters in the alert. The testimony showed that one plaintiff initially stayed in the car, and then in a hurried manner, ran into the store and confronted the other.

Fearing this suspicious behavior, Bart told you that he politely asked the Woodwards to come to the manager's office to talk. They agreed; who wouldn't? More good faith and good intentions all around. The testimony showed that the plaintiffs voluntarily went into the office. After the parties chatted, the police came and talked to them, and everyone left and went about their business. That was it. Not some federal case. Neither of the Woodwards testified that they ever told anyone that day that they wanted to leave or felt imprisoned.

The testimony showed no beatings, no guns, no rough stuff—just some conversation that was justified. The testimony showed no one was hurt, no one was put in prison, and no one is right 100 percent of the time.

The law says it is permissible for WelcomeMart to talk to the Woodwards when there has been suspicious behavior. The judge, when we are done talking to you, will instruct you on the law relevant to this case.

* * *

Good faith, good intentions, just plain bad timing. WelcomeMart ultimately filled the prescription. If things were that bad, why did the plaintiffs ultimately get the prescription filled at WelcomeMart?

We've all been the victim of bad timing, but the WelcomeMart employees were acting with good intentions. We respectfully ask you to return a verdict for the defendant WelcomeMart because the plaintiffs have not met their burden of proof. Plaintiffs have not proven their case by a preponderance of the evidence.

Thank you.

Next, Attorney Mighty delivers his closing for the plaintiffs:

Good afternoon, your Honor. Again, my name is Peter Mighty, and I will deliver the closing argument for the plaintiffs, Christopher and Mimi Woodward. May I proceed?

May I please use the enlarged exhibits to illustrate some points in my closing?

Was it just a dream that someday we would be judged not by what we look like or where we come from, but instead by the content of our character? The testimony shows that on June 11, when Christopher and Mimi Woodward entered that WelcomeMart store, they were judged not by the content of their character. Instead, they were targeted by the head of security at that store, Bart Harayda, and Officer Brayton simply because they were African-American. In doing that, the defendants violated laws against false imprisonment and the plaintiffs' right to be free from discrimination.

* * *

The Woodwards were profiled, pressured, and pained—profiled because they were African-American, even though the security advisory never mentioned the phrase "African-American." The testimony shows that the defendant WelcomeMart's employees—Bart Harayda, the head of security, and Shadique Brown, the store manager—as well as Officer Brayton of Nita City profiled the Woodwards because of what they looked like and what they wore. They pressured and pushed them into a tiny, hot, closed room to coerce them to confess to something the evidence indisputably shows they never did.

Christopher Woodward testified to going to the WelcomeMart store to have his prescription filled. He was falsely told that his insurance needed to be verified and he would have to wait. He waited politely. The store had the prescription that day, but its employees simply ignored it. The store's head of security, Harayda, sprang into action to send a message. As the evidence showed, he did so because he and the store's manager had established a profile of expected shoplifters: they were African-Americans wearing hooded sweatshirts—because, as Harayda said, that is what "those people" do.

Christopher waited patiently for his insurance to be verified, not knowing that was a lie. His concerned sister Mimi came into the store to look for him. Harayda and Officer Brayton grabbed the Woodwards and pushed them into that tiny, hot, confined space, threatening them to force them to confess to something they simply never did. In that tiny, hot, closed room the testimony proved that Harayda was irate and screamed at them: "I know you people. I am not going to let you leave until you tell me you took the drugs." And then he told them, "I will call the other police and have you arrested."

* * *

Profiled, pressured, and pained. And their pain and humiliation grew ever worse, particularly because of Christopher's recent surgery and Mimi's diabetic condition.

This abuse went on and on and on. Only when the police finally arrived were the Woodwards freed from their confinement in that tiny, hot, closed room. The testimony proves that any claim that the Woodwards stole anything that day is false. Even the defendant's own store manager said that the Woodwards stole nothing.

The Woodwards have proven their case by a preponderance of the evidence—and the judge will instruct you shortly that that simply means more likely than not, what they said was true:

1. The store agents and employees and Officer Brayton of Nita City profiled the Woodwards because they were African-American and dressed in sweatshirts. This is discrimination.

2. The Woodwards were pushed around and pressured in that room to confess to something that they simply did not do. This constitutes false imprisonment because they were intentionally confined against their will. The store clearly had no basis for this.

3. Because of their agents' disrespectful actions, WelcomeMart and the City of Nita inflicted horrible pain upon the Woodwards. It is this severe harm and discriminatory treatment that deserves just compensation.

When Christopher and Mimi Woodward walked into WelcomeMart that afternoon, they were not asking anyone to like or dislike them. All they asked was to be judged by their character. Harayda wanted to send a message to African-American people—and he did. However, we must reject the message of prejudice, profiling, and pressure. It must not go unchecked.

All the evidence leads to one and only one conclusion: you must send the defendants a message. The only true and just verdict finds the defendant liable for civil rights violations and the false imprisonment of Christopher and Mimi Woodward and awards the Woodwards the damages sought for their losses.

Thank you.

JURY INSTRUCTIONS

Next, the judge instructs the jury on the law. Earlier, attorneys for both sides submitted proposed jury instructions that they would like the jury to consider in its deliberations. Patty and Danny have both assisted their attorneys with finding jury instructions for the false imprisonment and civil rights claims. The attorneys revised and presented their instructions to the judge. Sometimes this happens at the start of the case, so the judge can consider those instructions while the case is proceeding, and other times it is just before closing arguments. The judge comes up with the proper instructions to submit to the jury and reads them to the jury.

Juries are usually made up of lay persons who may not understand or know the law that they are supposed to apply in the case, so the judge instructs the jury on the pertinent law. The jury will review the testimony and evidence to determine the facts—and whether, based on those facts, the law has been violated.

THE JURY'S VERDICT AND THE FINAL JUDGMENT

The jury deliberates, reviewing the testimony and evidence submitted and discussing the case in private throughout the afternoon. At one point, the jury foreman requests to see additional exhibits presented at trial, including Christopher Woodward's medical bills. After hours of deliberation, the jury reaches its verdict: they find for the plaintiffs on both the civil rights and false imprisonment claims.

Attorney Better makes another motion for judgment as a matter of law after the verdict. Again, he asks the judge to rule for the defendants—ignoring the jury's verdict—because he believes no reasonable jury should have ruled for the Woodwards based upon the testimony, evidence, and the law. After considering the motion, the judge denies it and enters judgment for the plaintiffs.

APPEAL

Attorney Better files his Notice of Appeal within the thirty-day limit, notifying the court and the plaintiffs that WelcomeMart intends to appeal the trial court's judgment in a federal appellate court sitting in the circuit that includes Nita City.

Large firms tend to have paralegals and lawyers who are more likely to specialize. Attorney Better and Danny work for a large firm, and they specialize in business litigation—they do not handle appellate work, which is handled by another attorney at the firm. Patty and Attorney Mighty, on the other hand, will continue to represent the Woodwards during the appellate process.

The appellant or petitioner—the party initiating the appeal—must assemble the trial record containing pertinent exhibits and file his appellate brief, a formal document that sets forth the legal arguments for reversing the trial court's decision. In this case, the new attorney handling WelcomeMart's appeal argues that the defendant's motions for judgment as a matter of law were erroneously denied by the trial judge and that the trial court erroneously permitted inadmissible hearsay evidence to be heard by the jury. The paralegal now handling the appeal ensures that a copy of the trial court's record—which contains the court record, trial transcripts, and evidence received at trial—is sent to the appellate court.

After the appellant's brief is filed by the new attorney handling the case, Patty begins researching past precedent to include in the Woodwards' response brief—the Woodwards will argue to the appellate court that the trial court's decision should be affirmed. She also helps Attorney Mighty draft the argument portion of the brief, and double-checks the rules of appellate procedure to make sure the brief meets format requirements.

Months after the briefs are filed, the parties are called for oral arguments in front of the appellate court. Unlike trial where testimonial evidence can take days, or even weeks to introduce, appellate oral arguments are much shorter—sometimes measured in minutes! The two attorneys argue their case to a three-judge panel of the appellate court and answer the judges' questions.

Months later, the court issues a judgment affirming the trial court's decision. Though WelcomeMart could potentially file a writ of certiorari and ask the United States Supreme Court to hear the case, the likelihood of certiorari being granted is slim because the Court receives many writs, but only hears a few of those cases each year. WelcomeMart decides not to pursue a further appeal and, after attempting to try and settle the case for less than the judgment amount, satisfies the judgment against it.

Q: What do you see as the litigation paralegal's role in the trial preparation process?

A: Answers provided by Janet A. Sullivan, Senior Paraprofessional Manager at Reed Smith, LLP and Beth Weller, Paraprofessional Coordinator at Reed Smith, LLP

[We] see them as a very integral part of the team and having an important role in coordinating all the aspects of preparing for a trial. Their role is to ensure that the trial team is prepared for and able to respond to any contingency that may arise before and during the trial. They provide a variety of organizational and substantive support. They are key players in providing logistical support in setting up trial workrooms, coordinating with witnesses and experts. They need to manage and track all the trial exhibits during trial, work with the court staff and court reporters.

Q: What are some of the typical tasks and responsibilities that your litigation paralegals handle?

A: • pleading preparation and filing;

• document retrieval;

• document production;

• indexing and coding;

• provide assistance in discovery matters;

• medical records review;

• preparation of chronologies;

• prepare subpoenas;

• schedule and prepare for depositions;

• prepare witness and expert binders;

- basic legal research;

- cite checking;

- create timelines and demonstrative exhibits;

- factual research;

- prepare appendices for briefs;

- assist in courtroom during trial;

- work with litigation support on technology for trials;

- and assist with appeals.

TO RECAP, LOOK AT THE FOLLOWING "TIMELINE" OR PROGRESSION OF PARALEGAL TASKS IN PREPARATION FOR TRIAL:

Stage 1: Intake

- Performing a conflicts search

- Putting together checklist of questions to ask before the initial client interview

- Doing preliminary research regarding the client's potential claims or defenses

- Conducting initial client interview or assisting attorney with conducting the interview

- Drafting intake memo

- Assisting the attorney with drafting intake documents, including contracts and letters of engagement

- Setting up new client file both electronically and in hard copy

- Setting up tickler system and inputting important deadlines

Stage 2: Preliminary Research

- Researching jurisdictional issues and local rules of procedure

- Conducting legal and factual research regarding the client's potential claims or defenses

- Assembling supporting evidence for claims and defenses

Stage 3: Settlement Issues

- Drafting demand letter
- Assisting the attorney in preparing for settlement conferences
- Investigating and verifying the client's claims and damages
- Assembling documents and other information supporting the client's claims and damages
- Drafting settlement brochure
- Keeping the client apprised of settlement matters

Stage 4: Filing Pleadings

- Assisting the attorney with choosing the proper forum
- Researching additional legal and factual issues regarding claims and defenses
- Drafting pleadings
- With proper supervision and signatures by the attorney, filing pleadings in court
- Assisting with service of process

Stage 5: Discovery and E-Discovery

- Coordinating deposition scheduling
- Coordinating materials for depositions and assembling documents that will be used during the deposition
- Assisting the attorney with drafting discovery requests and responses to requests
- Putting discovery information into databases and hard copy files
- Reviewing opponents' compliance, responses, and deficiencies, and addressing ongoing discovery and compliance issues as most local rules require
- Assisting the attorney with drafting and maintaining the privilege log
- Serving as the point person for discovery information, maintaining discovery databases electronically and in hard copy, and establishing the chain of command for discovery information

Stage 6: Pretrial Motions

- Performing legal and factual research to ascertain that the motion has factual and legal support

- Finding cases that are exactly on point

- Assisting the attorney with drafting motions and memoranda

- Assisting the attorney with obtaining witness statements and affidavits

Stage 7: Pretrial Conference

- Researching and coordinating facts and support for the pretrial memorandum

- Drafting the pretrial memorandum and coordinating any drafting and revisions necessary with the other side

Stage 8: Voir Dire

- Assisting the attorney with drafting questions and follow-up questions

- Researching local rules

- Making notes while the attorney is asking questions and relaying those notes to the attorney

Stage 9: Preparing Witnesses for Testimony

- Interviewing witnesses and gathering additional factual information

- Assisting the attorney with writing questions for direct and cross-examination

- Digesting depositions and key documents

- Assisting the attorney with gauging the witness's credibility

- Coordinating all supporting documents that the attorney will need in questioning and preparing the witness

- Serving as the contact person for the witness and increasing the witness's level of comfort

Stage 10: Preparing Exhibits and Demonstrative Evidence

- Getting documents and images assembled and making arrangements with outside providers for preparing exhibits and demonstrative evidence

- Assisting the attorney with planning the types of exhibits to be used, the information they will convey, and the costs to be considered

- Coordinating the use of technology in the courtroom and ensuring that all equipment and tools necessary for the attorney's presentation are available at the time they are needed

- Planning for some level of redundancy to ensure that backups will be available on any technology that is being used

Stage 11: Preparing the Trial Notebook and the War Room

- Assisting the attorney with planning the format, contents, and organization of the trial notebook

- Planning, organizing, and setting up the war room

- Assembling, organizing, and coordinating the documents that will go into the trial notebook and war room

- Maintaining the trial notebook and war room and updating them with any additionally discovered information

- Ensuring that the attorney has access to the trial notebook whenever she needs it

Stage 12: Trial Motions

- Performing legal and factual research to ascertain that the motion has factual and legal support

- Finding cases that are directly on point

- Assisting the attorney with drafting motions and memoranda

- Gathering the research and documents the attorney will need for trial motions

Stage 13: Assisting the Attorney at Trial

- Obtaining any documents, tools, and technology that the attorney may need at the trial

- Serving as the contact person for witnesses and others

- Coordinating witness scheduling and ensuring that all witnesses are ready and able to testify

- Ensuring that all exhibits are in place and available to use as needed during the attorney's presentation

- Taking notes at the trial

- Serving as an extra set of eyes and ears for the attorney to rely on

Stage 14: Posttrial Motions

- Performing legal and factual research to ascertain that the motion has factual and legal support

- Finding cases that are exactly on point

- Assisting the attorney with drafting motions and memoranda

Stage 15: Assisting the Attorney with the Appeal

- Obtaining the record

- Performing additional legal and factual research, including researching local appellate rules

- Assisting the attorney with drafting the appellate brief

- Assisting the attorney with preparing for oral arguments

TABLE 3.1: PERSPECTIVES FOR THE ATTORNEY-PARALEGAL TEAM

While your attorney is working on	You might assist by . . . .
• Establishing trial strategy	• Gathering factual and legal support for all the claims and defenses • Acting as a sounding board for various potential themes
• Organizing his presentation at trial	• Assembling the trial notebook and all supporting exhibits
• Determining what tangible and testimonial evidence to present at trial	• Providing for easy access and retrieval to information that is likely to be used during trial

KEY TERMS	
answer	memorandum of law
closing arguments	opening statements
demand letter	peremptory challenges
Federal Rules of Civil Procedure	pretrial conference
	request for the production of documents
FRCP Rule 12	voir dire
intake memorandum	witness examination
jury instructions	

DISCUSSION QUESTIONS

1. How would you have presented your opening statement to the jury?

2. What specific pieces of testimony would you have presented to make a compelling case for the plaintiffs? For the defendants?

3. Did everything in the case turn out as you expected? What were some of the parts of the story that surprised you?

4. What, if anything, surprised you about the role of the two paralegals in this case?

5. What would you have done differently to assist your attorney during trial?

6. Would you rather be working Patty's or Danny's job? Why?

PART II
PRACTICAL SKILLS

GETTING STARTED WITH CASE MANAGEMENT AND ORGANIZATION

This chapter describes methods of organizing and preparing initial documents, pleadings, pretrial motions, and correspondence. It also provides checklists and tips for setting up a new case file.

CHAPTER OVERVIEW

By the end of this chapter, you should be familiar with

- the process of setting up new case files;

- methods of organizing physical files;

- methods of organizing computer files;

- the elements of pleadings;

- the preparation of pleadings, pretrial motions, and other initial documents;

- drafting correspondence.

SETTING UP A NEW CASE FILE

When your firm takes on a new case, it may be the paralegal's responsibility to set up a new case file. Your firm may keep both hard-copy and soft-copy files (electronic or computer files) for each client and each case, and the hard-copy and soft-copy files will be cross-referenced.

A client file may have several components with separate folders for each, including

- Pleadings

- Correspondence

- Attorney notes

- Motions and responses to motions

- Discovery summaries

Some firms color-code their files so that each component of the file corresponds to a color—for example, all attorney notes may be done on blue paper. Color-coding not only makes for better organization and less confusion, but also may prevent the inadvertent release of privileged or confidential materials: if you know that confidential attorney notes are always on blue paper, you may be less likely to release something done on blue paper to someone outside the firm.

A thorough case file must contain a thorough index that lists all the file's components and all the documents that are stored in the file. Preparing and updating the index may be tasks that fall on the litigation paralegal. Updating the index is an essential task anytime a new document is introduced into the file or a current document is amended in any way.

Organizing Physical Files

Again, the method by which physical files are organized depends largely on the law firm, but clear, organized, and well-maintained files are a must for efficiently obtaining great results for your client. For some firms, alphabetical order makes sense—for example, a smaller firm that works generally on one matter for each client. Many firms use a numerical filing system, assigning client and matter numbers to each client. In our hypothetical example, the Woodwards may be assigned client number 056, and their suit against the pharmacy might be assigned matter number 001. So, all files pertaining to the suit would be filed under number 056-001. Your law firm should have an index of client and matter numbers that is kept electronically, easy to search, and updated regularly.

Paralegals must be vigilant about filing every document in the correct file. In litigation, organization and efficiency are everything—being able to find a document quickly and easily is essential. You must have a comprehensive understanding of how your firm's file system is set up and be able to retrieve documents quickly and efficiently.

Organizing Files Electronically

While law firms still use a lot of paper, much litigation material is now stored electronically. Some courts, including federal courts, require parties to file pleadings electronically; much discovery information is now found electronically or in computer databases; and most likely all correspondence, pleadings, motions, and other documents in the case will be saved on the firm's computers as well as stored in physical files. So, organized electronic filing is just as important—if not more so—as keeping your hard-copy files organized.

An electronic case file should be organized the same way as your hard-copy files: you should assign the same numbers to the file; you should keep the same folders; your index should be the same as the hard-copy index; and where applicable, the computer files should contain the same information as the hard-copy files. The databases will be arranged to make retrieval of the information fast and cost-effective. In many cases, the paralegal will be responsible for ensuring that discovery information is scanned into an electronic database, which will allow for efficient retrieval of the information.

DRAFTING PLEADINGS

Litigation paralegals are often involved with drafting the initial versions of pleadings. Of course, the paralegal's work must be closely supervised by the attorney—particularly when it comes to pleadings, which must be signed by the attorney and filed with the Court.

If you are asked to draft a pleading, first check your firm's database for sample forms. You do not have to reinvent the wheel in litigation: you can look up previous pleadings filed by your firm and follow their format. You can also turn to the law library for help: there are several litigation form books, such as the *Pleading & Practice Series* and *American Jurisprudence Legal Forms* that contain sample pleadings (though form books may vary by jurisdiction, and all forms must be adopted to the specific case and local requirements). Online legal databases such as Westlaw and Lexis also have sample litigation forms; in addition, there are state-specific litigation form books that can help you. Before you pick any one format to follow, be sure you double-check with your attorney to ensure you are using the right one for your case.

Each pleading will have several essential elements. A complaint will typically have a caption (which sets forth the jurisdiction, the court, the parties' names and designations, the name of the document, and the court's docket number, if available); a statement of jurisdiction (which sets out the basis of jurisdiction and venue in your forum court); a statement of facts; a statement of the plaintiff's claims; a prayer for relief (which is the plaintiff's request for judgment, damages, and other relief); and a subscription (which is the attorney's signature block). The answer will typically have the same caption as the complaint; an admission or denial of each claim in the complaint; a prayer for relief; and a subscription block. Answers may also contain affirmative defenses.

The following are some checklists to follow when drafting pleadings:

CHECKLIST 4.1: DRAFTING A COMPLAINT

Caption:

- Did you include the names and designations of the parties, the court, your jurisdiction, and the title of the pleading?

- Did you double-check jurisdictional requirements to ensure you are filing in the correct forum?

- Did you double-check format requirements to ensure you are complying with all local rules?

Statements of Jurisdiction and Venue:

- Did you name the parties and list their addresses (for individuals) or states of incorporation and principal places of business (for businesses)?

- If necessary, did you include a statement of subject matter jurisdiction?

- If necessary, did you include a statement of venue?

- If you are filing in federal court, did you specifically reference the court's basis for subject matter jurisdiction?

- Did you include all necessary introductory language?

Facts:

- Did you verify the facts before putting them in writing?

- Did you include the necessary facts?

- Did you ensure that your statements are factual and not legal in nature?

Claims:

- Did you include all of the various theories of liability in the counts?

- Did you include the necessary factual support and legal language on all of your counts to state a claim upon which relief can be granted?

- Did you remember to number all of your sections (jurisdiction, facts, and claims) properly?

- Did you remember to incorporate all previous paragraphs at the beginning of each new section as necessary?

Prayer for Relief:

- Did you ask for judgment for your client?

- Did you ask for all necessary damages, including punitive damages, costs, and attorney's fees where applicable?

- Did you request a jury trial where applicable?

- Did you ask the court for all other relief that the court may deem appropriate?

Subscription:

- Did you date your complaint?

- Did you provide a line for the attorney's signature?

- Did you include the name and designation of your party, as well as the attorney's name, address, contact information, and state bar identification number, as required by your forum court?

FIGURE 4.1: SAMPLE COMPLAINT

IN THE UNITED STATES DISTRICT COURT FOR
THE DISTRICT OF NITA CITY

CHRISTOPHER WOODWARD, MIMI WOODWARD	)	
	)	
Plaintiffs	)	**Civil Action No.**
v.	)	12-CV-2008-RWZ
WELCOMEMART, CORP., CITY of	)	
NITA and WILLIAM BRAYTON,	)	
Defendants	)	

COMPLAINT

Christopher Woodward and Mimi Woodward ("Plaintiffs"), by and through their undersigned counsel, hereby file this Complaint (the "Complaint"), pursuant to 28 U.S.C. 1983, 42 U.S.C. § 1981 and various state laws against WelcomeMart, Corp., and the City of Nita and William Brayton ("Defendants").

In support of this Complaint, Plaintiffs state as follows:

INTRODUCTION

This is an action to recover damages for violations of Plaintiffs' civil rights, their false imprisonment, and interference with their contractual relationships. The acts were caused and instigated by Defendant WelcomeMart, Defendant City of Nita, and Defendant Brayton. WelcomeMart acted by and through its agents, Bart Harayda, WelcomeMart's security guard, and Shadique Grayson, WelcomeMart's store manager, at the store owned and operated by the defendant at 131 Boulevard in Nita City, Nita. Harayda and Grayson were acting for the defendant and within the scope of their authority at all pertinent times. The Defendant City of Nita acted by and through its agent, Defendant William Brayton, who at the time of the acts complained of was on detail at the store and was acting for the City of Nita within the scope of his authority.

THE PARTIES

1. Plaintiff Christopher Woodward is a 28-year-old United States citizen of African-American national origin residing at 1 Main Street, Nita City, Nita.

2. Plaintiff Mimi Woodward is a 30-year-old United States citizen of African-American national origin residing at 1 Main Street, Nita City, Nita.

3. Defendant WelcomeMart, Corp. is a corporation organized and existing under the laws of the State of Nita with a principal place of business in Nita City, Nita.

4. Defendant William Brayton is a police officer employed by the City of Nita and residing at 25 Special Place, Nita City, Nita.

5. Defendant Nita City is a municipal corporation.

JURISDICTION AND VENUE

6. This Court, pursuant to 28 U.S.C. § 1331, has subject matter jurisdiction because Plaintiffs' claims are brought pursuant to 42 U.S.C. § 1981 for Defendants' violations of Plaintiffs' rights, and the Court has personal jurisdiction over the defendants.

FACTUAL ALLEGATIONS

7. Late in the afternoon of June 11, 2008, Mimi Woodward picked up her sibling, Christopher Woodward, from the oral surgeon's office where Christopher Woodward had just undergone oral surgery with Dr. Bhasin.

8. Dr. Bhasin prescribed to Christopher Woodward oxycontin and antibiotics to help ease the pain and fight infection. The nurse at the surgeon's office faxed the prescription to WelcomeMart.

9. Christopher Woodward walked into WelcomeMart and requested the prescription be filled.

10. The pharmacist and store manager Shadique Grayson said that Christopher Woodward would have to wait to get the prescription because the insurance needed to be verified. Christopher Woodward then decided to pick up a few items in the store.

11. Mimi Woodward entered the store shortly after Christopher Woodward. While walking toward Christopher Woodward, Mimi Woodward was accosted by security guard Bart Harayda. Harayda instructed Shadique Grayson to call out for the police officer on detail in the store, William Brayton.

12. Brayton ran to the aisle with his nightstick out and in an agitated state said, "You don't belong here, do you?" to Plaintiffs. Brayton and Harayda then forced the Woodwards into a small enclosed room at the front of the store. After locking them in the room, Brayton and Harayda confronted the Plaintiffs, and with their faces just inches from both Plaintiffs, Harayda yelled at them, "I know you took the drugs! I know you people! I am not going to let you leave until you tell me you took the drugs; then the other police will come and arrest you."

13. Mimi and Christopher Woodward informed Bart Harayda and Brayton that they had taken nothing. Brayton just laughed at them, and Harayda would not let them leave. Bart Harayda continued to question them, even as the room got very hot.

14. Mimi Woodward explained to Harayda about the surgery that had left Christopher in a great deal of pain. Harayda responded by saying, "I don't believe you people. I know the tricks you people use. I watch the news! Where do you keep your knives?"

15. After thirty minutes passed in the hot room, Shadique Grayson opened the door and informed Bart Harayda that the police from the local station were on their way.

16. Two more officers arrived and questioned the Woodward siblings. They concluded that nothing had been stolen and allowed the Woodwards to leave. Christopher Woodward left the store without picking up a prescription.

17. Christopher Woodward continued to suffer great pain and emotional distress in the days that followed this incident.

18. On July 1, 2008, Christopher Woodward was hospitalized with a serious staph infection and spent 10 days in the hospital on IV antibiotics.

19. Dr. Philip Saymort, Christopher Woodward's treating physician, continued to treat the Plaintiff for the next six months in order to restore the Plaintiff's health.

20. The treatment referred to in the two prior paragraphs was needed because of the Defendants' actions at WelcomeMart.

21. Christopher Woodward and Mimi Woodward lost wages, incurred significant medical expenses, and suffered severe emotional distress following the incident at WelcomeMart.

CAUSES OF ACTION

COUNT ONE

FALSE IMPRISONMENT

22. Plaintiffs incorporate Paragraphs 1 through 21 as if fully set forth herein.

23. Defendant WelcomeMart, by and through its agents Shadique Grayson and Bart Harayda, caused and forced Christopher and Mimi Woodward into a small room and locked the door, resulting in their involuntary confinement.

24. Defendants WelcomeMart, William Brayton, and City of Nita acted with the intent to confine both Christopher and Mimi Woodward until they confessed to crimes they did not commit.

25. Plaintiffs were aware of their confinement and knew of no reasonable or lawful way to break the confinement. As a result of the confinement, Christopher Woodward endured physical pain and suffering from not being able to take the prescribed medication to alleviate his pain. Mimi Woodward endured severe pain and suffering as a result of this confinement, because as a diabetic, Mimi Woodward's blood sugar levels dropped dramatically, causing migraines, blurred vision, fatigue, shooting pains in the abdomen, and risk of death.

26. Plaintiffs did not consent to the confinement. Defendants WelcomeMart and City of Nita, by and through their agents, forced Christopher and Mimi Woodward into the small confined space.

COUNT TWO

INTERFERENCE WITH CONTRACT BASED ON NATIONAL ORIGIN IN VIOLATION OF 42 U.S.C. §1981

27. Plaintiffs incorporate Paragraphs 1 through 21 as if fully set forth herein.

28. Plaintiffs are of African-American national origin, a recognized protected class under United States law.

29. Defendant, by and through its agents Shadique Grayson and Bart Harayda, intended to discriminate against Christopher and Mimi Woodward on the basis of national origin.

30. Defendant's discrimination interfered with Christopher Woodward's right to a contract with WelcomeMart for a prescription.

31. Defendants were acting under the color of state law when they treated the Woodwards in this discriminatory manner.

WHEREFORE, Christopher and Mimi Woodward demand a JURY TRIAL and pray that

1) Judgment be entered against all Defendants for all damages caused to Christopher and Mimi Woodward as a result of Defendants' conduct;

2) An award of punitive damages be issued against the Defendants;

3) Plaintiffs be awarded their costs and attorney's fees in this case;

4) Plaintiffs be awarded such other and further relief as this Court deems appropriate.

Dated: _____   Respectfully submitted by:

                                            _____

                                            Peter Mighty
                                            Attorney for
                                            Christopher Woodward
                                            and Mimi Woodward

156 Elm Street
Nita Town, Nita 55555

Registration #1234567

CHECKLIST 4.2: DRAFTING AN ANSWER

Caption:

- Did you include all necessary information in your caption, such as the names and designations of the parties, the court, your jurisdiction, and the title of the pleading?

- Did you include the requisite introductory language?

Jurisdictional Statements:

- Did you respond to all of the plaintiff's statements of jurisdiction and venue?

- Did you admit or deny whether jurisdiction and venue are proper?

Facts:

- Did you admit or deny each of the plaintiff's factual allegations?

- Did you clearly indicate in your answer where you have insufficient knowledge to either admit or deny the allegations?

Claims:

- Did you admit or deny each of the plaintiff's claims?

- Did you research the applicable law on the claims asserted?

- Did you remember to number all of your responses?

Affirmative defenses:

- Did you include any applicable affirmative defenses?

- Did you verify the factual details regarding the defendant's affirmative defenses before putting them in your answer as affirmative defenses?

- Did you include all necessary information that gives your client a legal basis for asserting their affirmative defenses?

Asserting Counterclaims:

- Did you research any legal claims your client may have against the plaintiff?

- Did you obtain needed verification and support for any counterclaim you may file?

- Did you assert each claim in sufficient factual and legal detail to withstand a motion to dismiss?

Prayer for Relief:

- Did you ask for judgment for your client?

- Did you ask for all necessary damages, including punitive damages, costs, and attorney's fees where applicable?

- Did you request a jury trial if applicable?

- Did you ask the court for all other relief that the court may deem appropriate?

Subscription:

- Did you date your answer?

- Did you leave a line for the attorney's signature?

- Did you include the name and designation of your party, as well as the attorney's name, address, contact information, and state bar identification number, as required by your forum court?

FIGURE 4.2: SAMPLE ANSWER

IN THE UNITED STATES DISTRICT COURT FOR
THE DISTRICT OF NITA CITY

CHRISTOPHER WOODWARD, MIMI WOODWARD))	
Plaintiff,)	**Civil Action File No.**
v.)	12-CV-2008-RWZ
WELCOMEMART, CORP., et al.)	
Defendants)	

ANSWER

COMES NOW Defendant WelcomeMart, Corp. (hereinafter "Defendant") and files this, its Answer to the Complaint of Plaintiff.

INTRODUCTION

Defendant admits that Bart Harayda is the security guard at the 131 Boulevard store location. Defendant admits that Shadique Grayson is the store manager and pharmacist at the 131 Boulevard store location. Defendant denies the remaining allegations set forth in the Introduction to the Complaint.

THE PARTIES

1. Defendant is without personal knowledge to admit or deny the allegations set forth in paragraphs 1, 2, 4, and 5 of the Complaint.

2. Defendant admits the allegations in paragraph 3 that it is a corporation organized and existing under the law of the State of Nita.

JURISDICTION AND VENUE

3. Defendant admits the allegations in paragraph 6 that jurisdiction and venue are proper.

FACTUAL ALLEGATIONS

4. Defendant denies the allegations set forth in paragraphs 7 through 21 of the Complaint because it is without sufficient knowledge to admit or deny the allegations.

CAUSES OF ACTION

COUNT ONE

FALSE IMPRISONMENT

5. Defendant denies the allegations set forth in paragraphs 22 through 26 of the Complaint because it is without sufficient knowledge to admit or deny the allegations.

COUNT TWO

INTERFERENCE WITH CONTRACT BASED ON NATIONAL ORIGIN IN VIOLATION OF 42 U.S.C. §1981

6. Defendant denies the allegations set forth in paragraphs 27 through 31 of the Complaint.

AFFIRMATIVE DEFENSES

Defendant relies upon the following affirmative defenses:

FIRST AFFIRMATIVE DEFENSE

The law allows Defendant to detain Plaintiffs for purposes of protecting the defendant's property and conducting an investigation.

WHEREFORE, having fully answered the allegations in Plaintiffs' Complaint, Defendant requests that the Court enter an Order dismissing the Complaint in its entirety with prejudice; awarding Defendant its costs and expenses, including reasonable attorney's fees; and awarding Defendant any other relief this Court deems just and proper.

Dated: _____   Respectfully submitted by:

_____

Joseph Better
Attorney for
WelcomeMart, Corp.

1 Financial Square
Nita City, Nita 55556

Registration #7654321

CORRESPONDENCE TIPS FOR PARALEGALS

Litigation paralegals are often involved with drafting and sending correspondence to clients, witnesses, opposing counsel, and others involved in a case. You may send enclosure letters with any documents or materials you send out; letters requesting information; letters providing information; or letters confirming information. In addition, you may send faxes or e-mails to clients and others.

Below are some general tips for drafting correspondence:

- Always use good grammar and spell-check everything—you are a professional; make sure your writing reflects that.

- Use your firm's letterhead and fax cover sheet where available. Many firms' fax cover sheets include a paragraph explaining the confidential nature of the information being transmitted.

- Use your firm's sample letters as examples of the letter format your firm would like you to use (there are several.) Typically, each letter should include the date of the letter, the recipient's name or address, a reference line, a salutation, the body of your letter, a brief closing, and a signature.

- Structure the body of your letter around the reason for sending the letter. For example, if you are sending enclosures, you may want to begin by describing the contents of your enclosures in one sentence; if you're requesting information, you may want to identify the information, your reason for the request, and the method by which you would like to receive the information. Keep your recipient in mind when you are writing to help you gauge the tone, formality, and language you should employ.

- Before you send the letter, double-check with your attorney to ensure you are not revealing any privileged or confidential information to someone outside of your firm.

- Check with your attorney about whether you or the attorney should sign the letter before you send it out. If you are signing the letter, be sure your nonlawyer status is listed below your name; also, if your name appears on the firm's letterhead, the ethics rules require that your nonlawyer status be listed there. If the letter provides legal advice or opinions, it is best that the attorney sign it; otherwise, the recipient may assume you are providing legal advice, which is something only attorneys are licensed to do. If the attorney is signing, be sure she oversees your work. Do not sign the letter with your attorney's name—if need be, sign your name and indicate that you are signing on the attorney's behalf.

- Proofread your letters again for content and grammar before you put them in the envelope.

- Be careful with what some see as more informal correspondence, such as e-mail. Proper grammar and spelling are still essential if you are going to be seen as a professional. If you are sending e-mails outside of your firm, you must still be cordial, formal when necessary, and careful not to divulge any privileged or confidential information. It is easy to get caught up in the immediate, informal tone of e-mail—so use the same tips for guidance before hitting "send" as you would before putting a letter in the mail.

FIGURE 4.3 SAMPLE CORRESPONDENCE

Small & Mighty, P.C.
156 Elm Street
Nita Town, Nita 55555

Peter Mighty, Esq.   *(555) 123-4567*

June 25, 2008

Christopher Woodward
77 Forest Street
Nita Town, Nita 55555

RE: Medical Records—Release Required

Dear Christopher:

Enclosed is a medical information and records release form, which requires your signature. Please sign and date where indicated and send the signed form back to our office as soon as possible.

Thank you for your prompt cooperation.

Very truly yours,

Patty Paralegal

Paralegal
/enc

Small & Mighty, P.C.
156 Elm Street
Nita Town, Nita 55555

Peter Mighty, Esq.   *(555) 123-4567*

Joseph Bigger, Esq.
Bigger & Better, LLP
75 Main Avenue
Nita City, Nita 55555

June 25, 2008

RE: Courtesy Copy of Complaint
     Woodward v. WelcomeMart, et al.

Dear Mr. Bigger:

Please find enclosed a courtesy copy of the Complaint filed in the above-referenced case in United States District Court for the District of Nita on June 24, 2008.

I will be making arrangements to have your client served, unless you would prefer to make arrangements to accept service of the summons.

I look forward to working with you to resolve this matter expeditiously.

Very truly yours,

Peter Mighty, Esq.

/PP
/enc

INTEROFFICE MEMORANDUM

To: Peter Mighty, Esq.

From: Patty Paralegal

Date: June 25, 2008

Re: Woodward v. WelcomeMart, et al.
        False Imprisonment Claim

ASSIGNMENT

You have asked me to find and analyze relevant legal authority regarding the Woodwards' false imprisonment claim.

ISSUE

Under Nita City case law, are the Woodwards likely to state a prima facie cause of action on their false imprisonment claim against WelcomeMart?

ANALYSIS

The court will address the Woodwards' false imprisonment claim using past precedent from state courts in our jurisdiction. I have found two relevant cases from courts in Nita City.

In *Smith v. MegaMart, Inc.,* 972 Nita 425 (Nita App. 1995), a Nita City appellate court held that the plaintiff stated a prima facie case where he was held by the defendant store in a storage room and interrogated by the store's security guard. In *Smith,* the plaintiff was suspected by the store's security guard of shoplifting a digital thermometer, but the court held that the defendant could not show that it was justified in holding the plaintiff.

Likewise, the defendant's motion to dismiss was denied in *Jones v. Hero Electronics,* 662 Nita 329 (D. Nita 2005), where the defendant store interrogated the plaintiff shoppers for two hours in a small room in the back of the store. The court in the *Jones* case held that the plaintiffs stated a case upon which relief can be granted and that the defendant could not show that it was justified in holding the plaintiffs captive.

The Woodwards' case is similar to the two cases above: they were also held and interrogated in a small room by WelcomeMart employees. Moreover, WelcomeMart likely cannot prove that the Woodwards did anything wrong while they were in the store. Based on the cases above, the Woodwards are likely to state a prima facie case of false imprisonment against WelcomeMart.

TABLE 4.1: PERSPECTIVES FOR THE ATTORNEY-PARALEGAL TEAM

While your attorney is working on	You might assist by . . . .
• Taking on a new client or a new case for an existing client	• Conducting the initial client interview or helping the attorney conduct the same • Drafting an intake memorandum • Setting up new electronic and hard-copy files for the case
• Filing the complaint	• Fact-gathering and legal research • Ascertaining that the claims have factual and legal support • Assisting the attorney with drafting the pleading • Obtaining checks for filing fees and filing the complaint
• Filing an answer	• Fact-gathering and legal research • Ascertaining that all defenses have factual and legal support • Assisting the attorney with drafting the pleading
• Filing a motion to dismiss	• Ascertaining that the motion has factual and legal support • Researching legal issues • Assisting the attorney with drafting the motion

• Moving for summary judgment	• Performing legal research and finding cases exactly on point • Gathering factual information and drafting and receiving affidavits from clients and witnesses
• Establishing a relationship with the client	• Assisting with or sending correspondence to the client • Contacting the client as requested by the attorney in order to relay or obtain information • Relaying the client's legal questions to the attorney
• Keeping the case organized and easily usable	• Organizing and maintaining hard copy and electronic files • Fully maintaining databases that will store information

KEY TERMS	
answer	cross-reference
caption	filing
case file	index
claims	pleadings
client/matter numbers	prayer for relief
complaint	subscription
correspondence	

DISCUSSION QUESTIONS

1. Suppose that the Woodwards decided to file suit only on their false imprisonment cause of action in your state's trial court.

   a. In what ways will the Woodwards' state court complaint differ from the sample federal court complaint in this chapter?

b. Draft a sample state court complaint on the Woodwards' behalf.

c. Draft a sample answer to the complaint you drafted in 1(b).

d. Draft a sample memorandum to your supervising attorney summarizing the research you have done on the Woodwards' false imprisonment claim, including cases from your state's courts.

INTERVIEWING AND INVESTIGATION

This chapter provides tips for investigation, record-gathering, locating witnesses, and interviewing clients and witnesses.

CHAPTER OVERVIEW

By the end of this chapter, you should be familiar with

- the types of interviews conducted by paralegals, attorneys, and law firms;

- essential interview skills;

- resources for locating people and information;

- tips for investigation;

- tips for formulating interview questions;

- the paralegal's role in preparing the client for testimony at trial or a deposition.

PARALEGALS AND FACT GATHERING

Fact gathering is an important part of the litigation paralegal's job. Paralegals often interview clients or witnesses or at least help the attorney prepare for those interviews. They often assist with investigation, record-gathering, and verification of records and other information as well.

INTAKE INTERVIEWS

Paralegals may conduct or otherwise be involved in the intake interview, which is the initial interview conducted with a new or potential client of the firm. During the intake interview, the goal of the paralegal is to get as much information from the client as possible—including personal and background information, facts about the client's case, information about what the client is seeking, and all records and documents the client has in his possession. At the end of an intake interview, the attorney may ask the paralegal to draft a memorandum—often called the intake memo—that summarizes the major facts and information the paralegal gathered from the client during the interview.

CHECKLIST 5.1: CONDUCTING AN INITIAL CLIENT INTERVIEW

Preparing for the Interview:

- Get as much information as possible about the reason for the client's visit to help you determine the types of questions to ask.

- Consult checklists and your attorney about what information you should be seeking from the client. Write out your questions ahead of time. If the attorney is conducting the intake interview, you may be asked to help come up with questions and then attend the interview and take notes.

- Make the client as comfortable as possible: greet the client in the waiting area; escort the client into your office; and offer a comfortable, quiet, and confidential place for the interview.

- Remember that new clients can feel uneasy when first coming into the office. For some clients, the mere idea of litigation or getting any kind of legal services is uncomfortable, while other clients are dealing with emotional cases or issues that make them nervous and anxious. Be personable and understanding during the interview, and briefly break the ice before you begin the interview.

Getting Personal and Background Information:

- Before the interview, check with your attorney about what types of personal and background information you need to get from the client, such as a history of prior litigation or criminal record. This may vary depending on the case or the client's story.

- If your firm has an established intake sheet, be sure you fill out all pertinent information.

- Do not forget the client's contact information—write down as many ways as possible to contact the client, from phone numbers to work addresses to online information.

Getting Information about the Client's Case:

- Let the client talk—avoid putting words in the client's mouth or asking questions that suggest the answer, particularly at the intake interview when you are hearing the client's story for the first time.

- Ask pointed and clear questions. Avoid asking multiple questions at once, and rephrase your questions as necessary if the client does not understand them.

- Ask follow-up questions on answers that need more clarification or may lead to additional important information. For example, if the client tells you that he is still in pain from his accident, ask for more details about the client's injuries, the extent of the pain and the injury, the medical treatment he has sought and received, and the medications he is taking.

- Ask the client for verification details, and ask the client to express how certain he feels about his description of the events.

- Remember to gauge your client's credibility during the intake interview. One of the functions of this interview is to help your attorney determine whether to accept representation. By making notes about the client's believability or trustworthiness, you can help the attorney gauge how well the case can be presented to the jury.

Getting to the Bottom of What the Client Wants:

- Walk away with a clear idea of what the client is seeking and what the client would like your firm to do in representing him. Note that clients sometimes do not know what they want—or, they may think they want one thing when their actual desired outcome is something completely different. It is important to understand the client's goals as early as possible.

Before You Send the Client Away:

- Double-check to make sure your pertinent questions have been answered.

- Verify all important information before the client leaves.

- Ask the client to provide you with any important information and records he has about the case (and if you have specific records that you know you will need, ask the client for those specifically). Also ask the client to sign any necessary releases, such as a release to obtain the client's medical files.

- If possible, let the client know what the next steps will be in the case and when he may hear back from the firm.

- Answer the client's questions if you can, but remember not to provide legal advice or relay any information that could be interpreted as applying the law to the client's specific situation. Relay all legal questions to the attorney and let the attorney answer them.

The following is a sample intake form, which was adapted from a sample form provided on the Maryland Bar Association's website. Note that your state or local bar association may likewise provide sample intake forms and other forms that you can modify and adapt for use in your own office.

FIGURE 5.1 INTAKE FORM

These questions will help us talk to you during your visit to our office. This information is confidential.

Name: _____
           Last   First   Middle

Address: _____
        Number   Street   City   State   Zip

Home Phone: _____ Cell Phone: _____

E-mail Address: _____

What do you need advice about or assistance with today?

_____

_____

_____

Briefly describe what happened:

_____

_____

_____

Who else do you know who was involved as either a party or a witness?

Party/Witness _____ Involvement _____

Contact Information _____

Party/Witness _____   Involvement _____

Contact Information _____

Party/Witness _____   Involvement _____

Contact Information _____

Party/Witness _____   Involvement _____

Contact Information _____

Party/Witness _____   Involvement _____

Contact Information _____

What papers or documents do you have or can you obtain that will help explain this situation?

    1. _____

    2. _____

    3. _____

    4. _____

    5. _____

What would you like to have happen on this matter?

_____

_____

Please check off the level of priority this matter has to you:

[ ]   Critical—Continuation of business or personal safety is involved.

[ ]   Very important—This matter poses a severe hardship.

[ ]   Important—Matter interferes with business or personal financial stability.

[ ]   Somewhat Important—Matter poses no immediate hardship.

[ ]   Interested—Interested in knowing my rights and perhaps interested in pursuing this matter further at some point.

Have you consulted any other attorneys on this matter? [ ] Yes [ ] No

If yes, what advice did they give you?

_____

_____

Have you ever been represented by an attorney before? [ ] Yes [ ] No

If yes, please state the circumstances:

_____

_____

How will you pay for your attorney's fees and costs in this matter?

_____

What is your full name? _____

Where were you born? _____

Are you known by any other names? [ ] Yes [ ] No

If yes, please give name(s):

_____

_____

Drivers License #: _____   Social Security #: _____

Where do you work? _____

How did you learn about us? _____

INTERVIEWING OTHERS

Paralegals may also assist the attorney with interviewing witnesses and others who may have information about the client's case. Because informal interviews are more cost-effective than formal discovery, attorneys will attempt to get as much information as possible through informal interviews and investigation.

The same considerations of thoroughness, preparedness, and professionalism apply to interviewing witnesses as to interviewing clients. You must get the gist of the witness's story, but while you are conducting the interview, you must also gauge the witness's credibility, depth of knowledge about the case, and ability to perceive.

Challenges may come up when interviewing witnesses and others—for example, you may encounter a witness who is refusing to cooperate or claiming that she does not have any information about the client's case. If this is the case, it is always better to stay pleasant and professional and attempt to get as much information as you can. You can try to appeal to the witness's sense of justice or explain that the more easily you can obtain necessary information, the less likely it will be for that witness to be compelled to testify. Still, at times, it may be necessary during litigation to use the court's subpoena power to compel the witness to attend a deposition or testify at trial.

PREPARING CLIENTS FOR TRIAL

Additionally, paralegals may be involved in preparing the client for testimony at trial or a deposition. This task also requires interviewing skills, but goes further than just getting information from the client: this interview assists the attorney with putting the client through a thorough direct and cross-examination and informs the client about what will take place at trial. Clients should not be surprised on the stand; they should be comfortable telling their story to the jury by the time it is their turn to take the stand. Clients are dealt a disservice if they are unaware of the process of direct and cross-examination and what will be required of them when they testify. The paralegal can play a key part in preparing the client for testimony.

CHECKLIST 5.2: PREPARING THE CLIENT FOR TESTIMONY AT TRIAL OR A DEPOSITION

Setting Up:

- Pick a location that will be similar to the courtroom (or in the case of a deposition, the office to be used.) In fact, if possible, go to an actual courtroom to prepare the client—some courts allow attorneys to use empty courtrooms, and law schools may also have a mock courtroom available.

- As always, consult litigation form books and your own firm's materials for checklists on questions to ask.

Getting Information from the Client:

- Use this interview to verify the details of the client's case as well as to plug any holes that may remain in the client's story.

- Continue to gauge the client's credibility as you go through this interview. Pay attention to how believable the client's story is and how it may be received by the jury. Always keep your attorney informed of any developments in this regard in order to avoid the highly damaging surprises that can occur at trial.

- Recognize wrong answers—for example, where the client contradicts an earlier version of the facts or changes his mind on his story.

- The client should be cross-examined by the attorney with the same questions that can be expected to come up on cross-examination at trial.

Providing Information to the Client:

- One of the most important functions of this interview is to provide the client with information about testifying at trial or a deposition. Remember, your goal here is to make the client comfortable with testifying at trial and to let the client know what he can expect when he takes the stand.

- First and foremost, tell the client that he must always tell the truth. Make sure the client understands the possible repercussions of perjuring himself on the stand and explain perjury to the client if necessary.

- Impress upon the client the importance of understanding a question before answering—if the client does not understand the question, he should ask the attorney to rephrase it.

- Tell the client not to volunteer information and only answer what was asked.

- Tell the client to be truthful and direct, and to use words he is comfortable with—the client should not sound like he has rehearsed his story over and over again, nor should he sound like someone he is not!

- Pay attention to how the client's story is coming across, and offer suggestions to the client on his tone, voice, presentation, and related matters.

Record Gathering and Verification

Paralegals also assist with investigation, record-gathering, and record verification. Property records, public records, financial records—these are just a few examples of information that paralegals may be asked to gather or verify in preparation for trial. To be effective at gathering or verifying records, you must be knowledgeable about the available sources of information (see the table 5.1 to give you some places to get started.) You must also understand which records are obtainable. In some cases, your firm may prefer to hire a legal investigator to help you find details about the parties, the witnesses, or the case. Because more and more information is found online, your investigation may start with a simple online search—a good search engine can be a paralegal's best friend in finding information for local and federal sources.

As with interviews, remember to be courteous, ethical, and professional when you are attempting to get access to information. You must make sure that you comply with federal and state privacy laws when attempting to gather or verify information. The federal Freedom of Information Act provides access to many sources of public records and information, but there are other federal and state laws that protect people from intrusions into their private information.

Table 5.1: Some Useful Sources for Research and Investigation

Source:	Where to find:	Type of information:
Social Security Administration	www.ssa.gov	Social security and disability information
Secretary of State's Offices	Check your local offices	Business filings and annual reports; state licenses
Internal Revenue Service	www.irs.gov	Taxes and related statements
U.S. State Department	http://www.state.gov/	International travel, visa, and business information
U.S. Military Records Office	http://www.archives.gov/veterans/military-service-records/	Military and veterans' records and statistics
U.S. Post Office	www.usps.com	Addresses, residency, and related information
U.S. Citizenship and Immigration Office	www.uscis.gov	Immigration information

Local police departments	Check your local offices	Police reports, arrest records, and related information
Municipal city halls	Check your local offices	Birth and death certificates, business licenses, marriage certificates, and other public records
Municipal assessors' offices or property records offices	Check your local offices	Property ownership records and related information
State registries or departments of motor vehicles	Check your local offices	Driving records, licenses, vehicle registrations, and related information
Public utilities	Check your local offices	Addresses, phone numbers, and occupants' names
Hospitals and medical offices	Check your local offices	Hospital and medical records
Schools	Check your local offices	School records
EDGAR	http://www.sec.gov/edgar.shtml	Securities and Exchange Commission filings and forms
Municipal voting lists	Check your local offices	Voting records
State registration boards for various professions	Check your local offices	Licensure and standing records, annual reports, and related professional information
GPO Access	www.gpoaccess.gov	Legislative materials, legislative, executive, and judicial resources
U.S. Patent and Trademark Office	www.uspto.gov	Filings and information on patents and trademarks
Administrative Office of the U.S. Courts, PACER Service Center	http://pacer.psc.uscourts.gov/	Federal court filings and documents

TABLE 5.2: PERSPECTIVES FOR THE ATTORNEY-PARALEGAL TEAM

While your attorney is working on	You might assist by . . . .
• Welcoming the client to the firm	• Researching legal and factual issues regarding potential claims and conflicts after the pre-interview • Preparing and reviewing checklists of questions to ask the client during the initial interview • Interviewing the client or assisting the attorney with the intake interview • Summarizing the intake interview into an intake memorandum • Tracking down information necessary for a final conflicts check
• Reviewing the results of the intake interview and researching facts that support the matter	• Investigating • Interviewing and locating witnesses • Making requests to get public documents
• Writing deposition questionsr	• Coordinating deposition scheduling • Coordinating the materials that the attorney wants the client to bring to the deposition • Assisting with the preparation of affidavits • Assembling and copying documents that will be used during the deposition

• Preparing the client or witness for a deposition	• Coordinating the materials that the attorney wants the client to bring to the deposition • Selecting documents from discovery that will be used during the deposition

KEY TERMS	
fact gathering	investigation
intake interview	privacy laws
intake memo	record gathering
interviewing	record verification

DISCUSSION QUESTIONS

1. Refer back to the fictitious case of *Woodward v. WelcomeMart.*

   a. What questions should Patty, the paralegal representing the Woodwards, ask her clients during the initial client interview? What types of records should she attempt to get from her clients and from other sources?

   b. What questions should Danny, the paralegal representing WelcomeMart, ask his clients? Who should Danny interview? What types of records should he attempt to get?

   c. Who might be some key witnesses to interview on both sides? What questions should the paralegals pose to the witnesses?

   d. How should Patty prepare the Woodwards for trial? What questions should she ask? What information should she relay?

KEEPING TRACK OF DISCOVERY
AND MASTERING E-DISCOVERY

Part of the litigation paralegal's job is to organize, categorize, and maintain discovery, as well as assist the trial lawyer with the discovery process. This chapter provides useful discovery and e-discovery tips.

CHAPTER OVERVIEW

By the end of this chapter, you should be familiar with

- how discovery and electronic discovery is conducted;

- what information can be stored electronically;

- tips for organizing, maintaining, storing, and updating discovery and e-discovery;

- the paralegal's role in conducting, managing, and maintaining discovery and e-discovery;

- discovery rules on electronically stored information.

AN INTRODUCTION TO CONDUCTING DISCOVERY

Effective and thorough discovery is the foundation of successful civil cases. Discovery is the formal process, in a civil suit, in which the parties exchange information and witnesses provide information. Paralegals play an important role in discovery. Paralegals need to know the methods of discovery and how to conduct discovery.

The main purpose of discovery is to gather information and evidence that you need to win your case. Effective discovery helps to avoid surprises at trial, narrow the issues to be tried, and preserve the testimony of witnesses who, for a variety of reasons, may not be available at trial. It also helps establish the testimony of unfriendly witnesses whose earlier statements can then be used to impeach them if they stray too far from their deposition testimony. Through effective discovery, you will help your attorney prepare for trial and dispositive motions to help gather information helpful to the client's case.

For example, in the case against WelcomeMart, the Woodwards may seek several documents from WelcomeMart: incident reports, company memos and directives for detaining suspected shoplifters, and memos dealing with employee training. WelcomeMart may seek the Woodwards' medical bills, medical opinions by experts, and even their prior criminal records.

The rules of civil procedure govern discovery. FRCP 26(b)(1) provides that

> Parties may obtain discovery regarding any nonprivi-leged matter that is relevant to any party's claim or defense—including the existence, description, nature, custody, condition, and location of any documents or other tangible things and the identity and location of persons who know of any discoverable matter. For good cause, the court may order discovery of any matter relevant to the subject matter involved in the action. Relevant information need not be admissible at the trial if the discovery appears reasonably calculated to lead to the discovery of admissible evidence.

The rules permit various methods of discovery. The principal method of discovery is done by asking people oral questions—depositions. The questions and answers are preserved, generally by means of a stenographer. Attorneys, with the help of paralegals, also propound interrogatories or depositions upon written questions to the opposing party or witnesses. These are written questions that must be answered under oath. Attorneys also issue requests for production of documents and things or issue subpoenas duces tecum for people to produce things within their possession. Paralegals work with their attorneys to write up questions and requests that are designed to elicit information that has a bearing on the case and that will be helpful in achieving a good outcome for the client.

The rules also permit a party to request that the opposing party or their agents undergo a physical or mental examination if the physical or mental condition of that person is in issue in the case.

A party may also submit requests for admissions to the opposing party. Requests for admissions are statements concerning facts and issues in the case and are designed to simplify the issues to be tried. Like much of the work done by the paralegal on any case, clarity in communication and collaboration with the attorney are the keys to assisting your attorney in conducting effective discovery.

For example, in the Woodwards' case against WelcomeMart, the Woodwards may request the following admissions:

- Admit that the Woodwards were lawfully on the premises.
- Admit that no stolen property was found on the Woodwards.
- Admit that WelcomeMart detained the Woodwards.

The person responding to the discovery request must be truthful. In addition to the penalties for committing perjury that are always present for untruthful statements made under oath to a court, the court may also impose sanctions on a party who does not cooperate with discovery or one who has been deliberately deceitful during discovery.

WHAT IS E-DISCOVERY, AND HOW IS IT CONDUCTED?

These days there is a vast amount of information stored electronically that must be obtained, preserved, documented, authenticated, and managed for use at trial. Many lawyers and paralegals who conduct discovery seek computer-generated or stored information for use as evidence at trial.

Think about your own course work. How much work do you do on a desktop or laptop computer? How many documents, photographs, and other pieces of information are stored on your desktop, laptop, and even your cell phone? When is the last time you sent a hard-copy letter to a friend or a loved one compared to an e-mail or instant message? Obtaining all that electronically stored information for a case is essential. As a paralegal, you need to know where information is likely to be located, the methods of retrieval, likely technological obstacles, and any cost constraints in obtaining that information.

It is vital in addressing e-discovery that you write proper requests in order to obtain all e-mail, work files, drafts of documents, text messages, and even IMs that may be related to issues in the case. It is common today to have more discoverable information stored electronically than in traditional paper files. That hastily written angry e-mail stored on the hard drive or thumb drive is more often the smoking gun found today. You need to ensure that you have taken steps in working with your attorney to uncover and preserve it.

Being technologically proficient is a good first step in the paralegal's development in creating and managing a successful e-discovery plan. Depending on the budget established for the case and your firm's in-house capabilities, it may be wise to consider engaging electronic discovery consultants, computer forensic investigators, or litigation support providers, who offer a wide range of support services including electronic document conversion, scanning, indexing, and online database management. In some cases, the firm may choose to engage an electronic discovery consultant to help create an effective strategy for collecting, analyzing, and processing the information. The scope of the consulting services can include assisting the team with preparing discovery requests, reviewing and evaluating discovery responses, shaping arguments against overly broad or costly discovery requests, and supporting the collection, analysis, and production of responsive electronic information.

In dealing with electronic discovery, the paralegal should be thoroughly familiar with the essential technological terms. In this way, you can seek specific information and respond to the opposing party's request for information with clarity. You need to know where to find computer-related evidence and when to consider making the use of outside experts to assist with e-discovery and computer forensics. In this way, you can ensure that you have sought out all sources for potential evidence. In conducting e-discovery, the same methods of traditional discovery are employed—requests for production of documents and things or subpoenas duces tecum with a notice of deposition—and the key is to ensure that a detailed search for hard-copy and soft-copy information was conducted. Paralegals, working with their attorneys, should write detailed questions so the person responsible for providing information can be asked specific questions regarding where she searched for information, what databases she examined, and what devices (including portable devices) she searched to find information and data responsive to those requests.

THE PARALEGAL'S ROLE IN CONDUCTING AND MAINTAINING DISCOVERY AND E-DISCOVERY

Paralegals play an important part and various roles in conducting and maintaining discovery information and electronically stored information. They assist the attorney in obtaining documents and information from the other side; they also assist the attorney with gathering information and documents from the client in response to discovery requests. From identifying the information that needs to be obtained to maintaining and managing discovery and e-discovery as the firm obtains it, paralegals are integral to the formal process of exchanging information and documents in a case.

The paralegal's task during discovery is to gather efficiently the relevant information needed for your litigation team to be successful. You may be asked to:

- Create a master discovery management plan that will include scheduling depositions of witnesses, gathering documents and evidence, and establishing a budget for discovery.

- Create a specific e-discovery management plan that addresses the source and location of information and addresses both the legal and technological challenges that will need to be overcome.

- Establish benchmarks, timelines, and goals that fit within your overall case strategy and budget.

- Write clear discovery requests that your attorney can review and submit to the opposing party for response.

- Effectively track the progress of the discovery efforts and your team's discovery obligations.

- Successfully collect, preserve, and analyze key information gathered during discovery and e-discovery, and then cull essential information into a useable database.

CHECKLIST 6.1: CONDUCTING DISCOVERY AND E-DISCOVERY

Typical paralegal tasks in conducting discovery and e-discovery include:

- Meeting with your attorney early on to discuss what documents are relevant and need to be obtained and to discuss general strategies for obtaining the necessary information.

- Identifying the documents that need to be obtained;

- Identifying the people and sources from which those documents need to be obtained;

- Identifying the formats in which the information will be provided, and identifying and obtaining any technology necessary to process those formats;

- Creating a formal project plan (along with appropriate deadlines) for obtaining all discovery information;

- Pinpointing the costs that will be involved with discovery and e-discovery, and assisting the attorney with sorting out who will bear the burden of those costs;

- Obtaining cost estimates from the client and outside providers, and assisting with the creation of a discovery and e-discovery budget;

- Assisting the attorney to comply with discovery requests from the opposing party.

CHECKLIST 6.2: MAINTAINING AND MANAGING DISCOVERY AND E-DISCOVERY

Typical paralegal tasks in maintaining and managing discovery and e-discovery include:

- Assessing and obtaining the tools necessary to store information in an organized, effective, and secure manner;

- Entering (or assisting others with entering) information into the appropriate databases and hard-copy files;

CHAPTER 6

- Creating appropriate indexes and cross-indexes;

- Taking precautions to ensure that discovery and e-discovery will be kept secure;

- Creating privilege logs;

- Facilitating communication and cooperation between the attorney, the client, and any outside providers involved;

- Keeping track of additional information that needs to be obtained.

TABLE 6.1: PERSPECTIVES FOR THE ATTORNEY-PARALEGAL TEAM

While your attorney is working on	You might assist by . . . .
• Drafting or reviewing requests for admission and interrogatories	• Assisting with drafting documents • Organizing responses received • Putting information into databases
• Preparing to conduct depositions	• Sending out deposition notices and subpoenas • Scheduling witnesses and a stenographer/videographer • Double-checking factual support and ensuring that supporting documents are available for the attorney to use at the deposition
• Ensuring that discovery remains organized and easily accessible	• Setting up discovery databases, both electronically and/or hard copy • Setting up index and cross-index systems • Establishing a chain of command for the person who obtains, organizes, and maintains discovery documents

• Preparing discovery motions or letters to the opponent addressing outstanding discovery issues	• Assisting with drafting motions, memoranda, or letters • Performing legal research on dispositive cases dealing with relevant discovery issues

KEY TERMS	
complying with discovery discovery discovery requests e-discovery	electronically stored information motion to compel sanctions

DISCUSSION QUESTIONS

1. In what ways are paralegals integral to the process of conducting, organizing, maintaining, and updating discovery, e-discovery, and electronically stored information? What are some typical paralegal tasks in this regard?

2. Refer back to the case of *Woodward v. WelcomeMart*.

   a. Name some examples of discovery requests that each party may submit to the other side. Then, draft a sample discovery request on behalf of the Woodwards.

   b. What types of information may be stored electronically in the case? What are some examples of electronic discovery that may come up?

   c. What tasks may paralegals Patty and Danny be involved in while conducting discovery and obtaining information from the other side?

   d. What precautions can Patty and Danny take to make sure discovery and e-discovery are properly managed and maintained?

E-DISCOVERY ISSUES AND PROGRAMS

This chapter discusses the issues and technical and organizational problems and solutions available for handling e-discovery, the discovery of electronically stored information (ESI), as well as the paralegal's role in helping attorneys comply with e-discovery matters.

CHAPTER OVERVIEW

By the end of this chapter, you should be familiar with

- e-discovery compliance issues;

- electronic information storage, retrieval, and methods of production;

- the technical and organizational problems and solutions available for handling e-discovery;

- the paralegal's role in e-discovery retrieval and organization;

- the paralegal's role in helping attorneys comply with the rules on e-discovery.

First, let's take a step-by-step look at the major e-discovery steps involved in litigation:

Step 1: Spoliation Matters.

A litigation hold preventing the recycling, discarding, or deletion of electronically stored media and information is established when litigation is reasonably anticipated, but no later then when you have notice of pending litigation. This is an important step in preserving information so that it is available for discovery, as many businesses and individuals routinely recycle their backup media and delete material in the ordinary course of business. Establish a litigation hold at the earliest possible opportunity in order to avoid claims of spoliation of evidence.

Step 2: Discovery Sources.

Your litigation team determines likely sources of discoverable information, both from a standpoint of key people and of repositories for such information.

An organizational chart and schematic for stored information helps pinpoint likely targets for e-discovery and traditional hard-copy material. These issues are discussed both with the client—who will need to conduct searches responsive to the adversary's requests—and with opposing counsel, to narrow areas of dispute and speed discovery.

Step 3: Initial Disclosures.

Federal courts require the parties to make initial disclosures before formal discovery can be undertaken. Some state courts require the same. As part of the initial disclosures in accordance with Rule 26(f), the parties put forward a plan for dealing with e-discovery issues, including the discovery of electronically stored information from sources that the party identifies as not reasonably accessible because of undue burden or cost. On a motion to compel discovery or for a protective order, the party opposing the discovery must show that the information is not reasonably accessible because of undue burden or cost. The discovery plan must state the parties' views and proposals on any issues about disclosure or discovery of electronically stored information, including the form or forms of production and any limitations on discovery.

Step 4: E-Discovery Plans.

The court may issue discovery orders regarding the plan or require a formal discovery conference or pretrial conference under Rule 16, which will set out timelines, the scope of discovery including e-discovery, and software and expense issues concerning e-discovery.

Step 5: E-Discovery Searches.

Your litigation team drafts discovery requests, including interrogatories and requests for production of documents, targeting the identity and holders of key electronic and other information that falls within the scope of discoverable information. Your team drafts search terms to use in e-discovery, including key term, key concept, and fuzzy search requests (explained further below). At this point, a "keeper of the records" deposition is scheduled to ensure that all possible sources of discoverable information have been reached.

Step 6: Discovery Compliance and Privilege.

Your litigation team reviews responses from the client and opponents to ensure compliance with the discovery requests, assertion of privilege claims, creation of a privilege log, and any objections to the requests. A party produces a privilege log when objecting to a discovery request based on privilege or work product. The privilege log briefly describes each document that is protected by a claim of privilege or other protection while being careful to preserve the privileged contents. The person asserting the privilege generally provides the following information in the privilege log for each document: the author or authors, the recipient or recipients, its date or dates, its length, the nature of the document or its intended purpose, and the basis for the objection. The privilege log is served on all other parties, who may then object to any asserted claims of privilege. The procedure for production of a privilege log and contesting its claims are more often found in case law than in the rules of civil procedure. Objections to discovery requests are made for a variety of reasons: the requested information exceeds the scope of permissible discovery; the time period is too broad; the cost of search and retrieval of e-discovery information is too expensive and therefore should be borne by the requesting party; and the information is available on stored media that is simply too expensive or inaccessible to retrieve.

Step 7: Discovery Compliance Conferencing.

Good practice demands—and many local rules require—that discovery issues be discussed by counsel before presenting them to the court for resolution. Whether it is e-discovery or traditional discovery issues, this "meet and confer" practice helps narrow the area of dispute and may help reduce the cost of final compliance. Some courts also require the parties to formally meet in person and confer before filing Rule 37 motions.

Step 8: Seeking Sanctions.

Under Rule 37, the litigation team prepares and presents motions to the court to resolve outstanding e-discovery and other discovery compliance issues.

TECHNICAL AND ORGANIZATIONAL PROBLEMS AND SOLUTIONS FOR HANDLING E-DISCOVERY

In this electronic age, discovery—and specifically the discovery of ESI—is a tripartite problem involving information storage, data retrieval, and methods of production. Each part of the puzzle has its own problems and pitfalls, and the paralegal must be knowledgeable about where data is stored, how it is retrieved, and how it can be produced in a cost-effective manner.

It is vital that while handling ESI, you ensure that attorney-client privilege is not lost through inadvertent disclosure of protected information. The attorney-client privilege protects the exchange of confidential information between the attorney and the client. Its objective is to encourage an open and honest exchange of information between the attorney and the client, thus allowing the client to provide the attorney with information knowing that the attorney will protect the secrecy of that information, and allowing the attorney to provide important and needed advice to the client. The work-product privilege likewise can prevent the disclosure of material that an attorney possesses that was created on a client's behalf in anticipation of litigation or for trial. It includes information from witnesses, investigative reports, and even the attorney's mental impressions and strategies.

In order to provide a consistent standard for application of the attorney-client privilege and work-product doctrine and address the increasing costs of litigation connected with these issues, Rule 502 of the FRE was amended to provide for remedies for the inadvertent disclosure of protected information, especially concerning ESI. The stark increase in discovery materials related to ESI has led to dramatic litigation cost increases and additional burdens on the courts. It is now less complicated to resolve privilege disputes for more broadly defined covered material and for materials inadvertently disclosed.

A reasonable effort to maintain privilege must be undertaken during production of ESI; it is likely then that the court will find that the attorney-client privilege has not been lost even though documents may have been inadvertently disclosed.

Identifying repositories of likely sources of information is the first step in undertaking a thorough search for ESI. Repositories of electronicly stored information include computers, file servers or other network interfaces, backups, disks, tapes, CD/DVDs, electronic devices, cell phones, or other storage media. A thorough list of these storage media must be made—both for information you will be asked to produce and for information you are seeking from the opponent.

Once you have established with your attorney and IT expert the likely repositories of information, it will be necessary to prepare your discovery requests and ensure that they are sufficiently encompassing to sweep in the necessary information to prove the case. Sampling is often used in searching repositories for ESI. It is used to test databases for the existence and amount of relevant information. Sampling helps finalize decisions about which repositories of data are likely to yield discoverable information and the likely effectiveness of such searches or other data extraction procedures.

In searching for ESI, your team must adopt a search methodology that will identify potentially relevant electronic documents reliably and efficiently. This task requires subject matter and technological and legal expertise, and it needs to be undertaken in cooperation with your attorney and office IT specialist.

Keyword searches search for a term exactly as the search term specifies, so a keyword search will not pick up documents containing abbreviations or common misspellings. To locate such information, you will need to perform additional keyword searches or fuzzy searches. Fuzzy searches are searches conducted for misspelled terms and concepts and are helpful in returning results when the original text has been corrupted through an optical character recognition error common in scanned documents. Boolean searches search for terms appearing in a specified relation to one another, usually with connectors like "and," "or," and "but not." Courts often accept as appropriate either or both search methodologies. Other search methodologies gaining in use are content-based searches, which identify and organize concepts into clusters, or concept-based searches, which broadens a keyword-based search to include synonyms or related concepts. Clustering is a statistical analysis of ESI, which identifies relationships among documents that have similar content and clusters the identified information together.

Once information is found in the storage media, the method of production becomes the paramount issue. If there is only a little information in a readily available program, it can be loaded onto a CD or DVD at relatively little cost and provided to the opponent. That, however, is not often the case. While the cost of the search in work hours can be an expensive endeavor, the cost of retrieval on backup or stored media can be even more expensive, especially in a case involving voluminous information. If the information requires an expensive or hard-to-locate program or application in order to retrieve or view the information, the cost of e-discovery increases. The court can order the sharing of expenses associated with e-discovery.

There are also software applications and ESI providers that help ease the burden of e-discovery. A good e-discovery program automates the discovery of information, thereby making large batches of electronic databases, documents, and e-mails easily accessible for search and review by attorneys and paralegals. The software accelerates document processing, allowing users to gain immediate review of the facts; conduct e-discovery searches; group documents together by discussion threads and concepts; and receive comprehensive case management support. The following are some examples of programs and ESI support providers used by law firms and attorneys:

- Software programs like Kazeon, CommVault, Guidance, and i365 cover all of the stages of e-discovery and emphasize e-discovery and document management.

- Others, such as Assentor, Attenex, Autonomy, CaseLogistix, Cataphora, Stratify, and Zantaz include advanced concept searching and analytics to streamline the review process.

- HardCopy Pro Plus is an application for data discovery, used in conjunction with retrieval systems to make large batches of electronic documents and e-mails easily accessible for searching and review.

- iLumin Software Services Assentor Discovery 2.0 is a tool for rapidly searching and producing e-mail messages. Assentor Discovery provides the ability to harvest archived information and manage and produce that information or preserve it for protection by the attorney-client privilege.

- Stratify Legal Discovery service is a full service ESI and e-discovery processing service; it culls the data universe and statistically analyzes terms and phrases, both within and across documents in responding to or reviewing responses to discovery requests.

- Williams Lea, Inc., is a national company that provides e-discovery services, reprographics, imaging, and digital processing services to law firms and attorneys.

- DiscoverReady LLC is a national provider of discovery management and document review services to Fortune 500 corporate legal departments.

- Fios is an electronic discovery services provider that manages every aspect of discovery response enabling collection, processing, review, and delivery of relevant documents in a predictable and legally defensible manner. Supported by Fios, DiscoveryResources.org is an online resource for law firms and litigation support professionals seeking current information about electronic discovery.

- Kroll Ontrack provides corporations, law firms, and government agencies with technology and consulting services for large-scale paper and electronic discovery, computer forensics, and litigation readiness and response projects.

- eClaris is an e-discovery consulting firm that assists law firms and corporations with classifying, processing, and reviewing their electronically stored data.

Concerned with the rising costs associated with e-discovery because of the serious burden it places on the judicial system, the Sedona Conference launched a national drive to promote open and forthright information sharing, training, and the development of practical tools to facilitate cooperative, collaborative, transparent discovery. The Sedona Conference is a good source of information on the latest trends in e-discovery. It is developing and distributing practical "toolkits" to train and support lawyers, judges, paralegals, and others in techniques of discovery cooperation, collaboration, and transparency. It is creating a clearinghouse of practical resources, including form agreements, case management orders, and discovery protocols.

Two particularly useful sources of information for "best practices" regarding the methodologies of searching are *The Sedona Conference® Best Practices Commentary on Search and Retrieval Methods*[1] (August, 2007) and the federal government's Text Retrieval Conference ("TREC") Legal Track[2] initiative. The Legal Track at the Text Retrieval Conference assesses how effective the comparative search methodologies are at retrieving information. The TREC Legal Track was held for the first time in

---

1. *Available at* www.thesedonaconference.org/difForm?did=Best_Practices_Retrieval_Methods_revised_cover_and_preface.pdf (last visited May 13, 2009).

2. *Available at* http://trec.nist.gov/ (last visited May 13, 2009).

2006 and is in the process of establishing objective benchmark criteria for comparing search technologies.

ESI TERMINOLOGY FOR THE PARALEGAL

There are some fundamental terms that the paralegal must know when dealing with ESI:

- Attachments. These are electronic files appended to e-mails.

- Backup. Backup is the copied file that results from the activity of copying files or databases to preserve access to the information in case files are lost or corrupted due to operator error, equipment failure, or other problems. Most businesses and individuals create backups routinely. Backups are a source of locating discoverable information even when an attempt has been made to destroy the information.

- Computer Forensics Specialist. This is a computer investigation and analysis expert who searches for concealed or "lost" information that may be recovered from the computer. Computer forensic specialists use many methods to capture computer system data and recover deleted, encrypted, or damaged file information.

- Computer Network. This is a series of computers connected to a server or host computer that stores files for access by other computers on the network.

- Data Filtering. Data filtering is the process of identifying and extracting data based on specified limitations such as keywords, file types, dates, or names.

- Deleted files. File are deleted from an operating system for various reasons, but even deleted files can sometimes be recovered and restored to the computer.

- E-mail thread or e-mail string. This refers to e-mails linked together by e-mail responses and forwards.

- E-Discovery. This is the search, retrieval, collection, review, and production of electronically stored information (ESI) in discovery. This includes all "soft-copy" information, as opposed to paper copies, which are traditionally called "hard-copy" material.

- Electronically Stored Information (ESI). These are files or other data that are stored on computers, file servers, disks, tapes, or other electronic devices or media.

- File Server. A file server is a host computer that stores files for access by other computers on a network of computers.

- Fuzzy Search. Fuzzy searches are searches conducted for misspelled terms and concepts. Fuzzy searches are helpful in returning results when the original text has been corrupted through an optical character recognition (OCR) error, which is common in scanned documents.

- Harvesting. Harvesting is the practice of retrieving electronic data from computers and other storage media.

- IT Specialist. This information technology professional provides technical and consultative expertise in the support and coordination of computer hardware, software, information, technology services, and activities.

- Legal Hold. A legal hold is a notice or communication from counsel that suspends the normal document retention policy, such as the deletion of old files and the disposition or processing of records like backup tape recycling.

- Metadata. Metadata is information about the characteristics, origins, or usage of an electronic file embedded in the file. This information is not visible when viewing a printed or on-screen rendition of the document. Metadata is either application metadata, which is information not visible on the printed page but embedded in the document file; or system metadata, meaning data stored externally on the computer file system.

- Native File Format. These are electronic documents produced as originally maintained and used in the application.

- Optical Character Recognition (OCR). This is the process of scanning images and electronically converting them into editable text.

- Outlook. Outlook is Microsoft's personal information management (PIM) program, which includes e-mail, task management, and calendar.

- Portable Document Format (PDF). This format preserves the fonts, images, graphics, and layout of the source document in an electronic format. PDF files are viewed and printed with Acrobat, a viewer application available from Adobe Systems.

- Privilege log. A party produces a privilege log when objecting to a discovery request based on privilege or work product. The privilege log briefly describes each document that is protected by a claim of privilege or other protection while being careful to preserve the privileged contents.

- PST file format. File format used by the personal information management (PIM) program of Outlook, which includes e-mail, archived e-mails, task management ticklers, and a calendar.

- Sampling. Sampling is the process of testing a database for the existence or frequency of relevant information.

- Spoliation of Evidence. Spoliation concerns the destruction, loss, or alteration of data or documents that could be evidence in litigation. Some jurisdictions have a separate cause of action for spoliation of evidence in addition to other remedies plaintiffs may invoke.

- TIFF or TIF. TIFF stands for Tagged Image File Format. This is an electronic copy of a document in the form of an image. TIFFs do not retain metadata from a source electronic document.[3]

DISCOVERY RULES FOR ELECTRONICALLY STORED INFORMATION

The Federal Rules of Civil Procedure recognize that much information is stored electronically, and the rules regulate the maintenance and discovery of electronically stored information, or ESI. This means that attorneys, paralegals, and clients must be thoroughly familiar with the obligation to retain and retrieve information created, stored, or in any way associated with a computer whether presently involved in litigation or not. You must also know how to obtain ESI in the hands of your opponent. The advocate, paralegal, and client must also ensure that the company's e-mail and document retention policies do not conflict with the obligations of companies to preserve information.

Obligations to protect electronic information reach beyond the rules of civil procedure and extend to counsel as evidenced by the indictment of a lawyer in Connecticut for violating the Sarbanes-Oxley Act, 18 U.S.C. § 1519 (relating to the destruction, mutilation, or concealment of records) for his role in dismantling his client's laptop. The attorney ultimately pleaded guilty to misprision of a felony.[4]

The modern Federal Rules of Civil Procedure for electronic discovery change little the discovery practices that most lawyers have engaged in for years. While there are now additional obligations on counsel to educate clients and preserve information, and concomitantly additional expense, these rules merely reflect how our business and social culture have changed because of the desktop computer. For many years now, the smoking gun in any case was more often found on an opponent's hard drive than in yesterday's hard-copy format. Business organizations have a near universal reliance on electronic records, and good discovery practices recognize that practice. The changes to the Federal Rules of Civil Procedure in 2006 simply reflect our growing reliance on ESI.

---

3. Lexbe, *e-Discovery & Metadata Definitions*, http://www.lexbe.com/hp/define-e-Discovery-metadata.htm (last visited May 13, 2009).

4. USA v. Russell, No. 3:07-CR-00031, 2007 WL 4961124 (D. Conn 2007).

Lawyers issue broad requests for all relevant documents including hard copy and electronic ones in "soft copy." It is important to note that information received and produced in discovery may need to be put in a usable format with the applicable programs. Under the rules of civil procedure and case law, the production of ESI is a cooperative endeavor, which may include the sharing of resources and costs.

CHECKLIST 7.2: THE PARALEGAL'S ROLE IN COMPLYING WITH RULES REGARDING E-DISCOVERY:

Working with your attorney, you must ensure that you and the client:

- Give early attention to issues relating to electronic discovery, including the form of production, preservation of information, and problems reviewing electronic information for privilege.

- Make a diligent search for ESI while recognizing that the cost of searching for inaccessible electronic information may need to be addressed by the court.

- Are careful not to disclose privileged information that is stored electronically while recognizing that information inadvertently disclosed may retain protection if the privilege is asserted reasonably after the inadvertent disclosure.

- Work on an agreement regarding the form of production of electronic information or present the issue promptly to a judge for determination.

- Avoid court-imposed sanctions for the deliberate loss of electronic information. If you can show that the routine operations of computer systems, such as the automatic purging of stale e-mails, caused the loss, then you may avoid potential sanctions.

The major rule requirements regarding the discovery of ESI are found in the requirements of Rules 16(b) and 26(f) pertaining to counsel's obligation to meet and confer; Rule 26(b)(2), regarding the duty of disclosure; Rule 26(b)(5), relating to privilege claims; Rule 34, concerning the different forms of production; and Rule 37, and its safe harbor provisions; as well as sanctions, for the loss of certain ESI.

Many district courts have local rules addressing electronic discovery, therefore it is especially important to review these rules with your attorney as you undertake discovery. Some courts have fashioned sample discovery plans that you should review with your attorney and discuss how he would like you to proceed. Many of these sample discovery plans include provisions for electronic information disclosures. These discovery plans often require the parties to provide a brief description of their proposals regarding the disclosure or discovery of electronically stored information, identify any disputes regarding the same, and include a proposed order.

FIGURE 7.1: SAMPLE DISCOVERY PLAN

The United States District Court for the District of New Hampshire offers the following sample discovery plan on its website:[5]

UNITED STATES DISTRICT COURT
DISTRICT OF NEW HAMPSHIRE

Plaintiff(s)	)	
v.	)	**Civil No. Case #**
	)	Judge Initials _____
Defendant(s)	)	

DISCOVERY PLAN

FED. R. CIV. P. 26(F)

DATE/PLACE OF CONFERENCE:

COUNSEL PRESENT/REPRESENTING:

CASE SUMMARY

THEORY OF LIABILITY:

THEORY OF DEFENSE:

DAMAGES:

DEMAND:

    due date [need not be filed with the court]

---

5. *Available at* http://www.nhd.uscourts.gov/ru/form-samplediscoveryplan.asp (last visited May 14, 2009).

OFFER:

due date [need not be filed with the court]

JURISDICTIONAL QUESTIONS:

QUESTIONS OF LAW:

TYPE OF TRIAL:

Jury or Bench

DISCOVERY

TRACK ASSIGNMENT:

EXPEDITED—6 MONTHS

STANDARD—12 MONTHS

COMPLEX—24 MONTHS

DISCOVERY NEEDED:

Give brief description of subjects on which discovery will be needed.

MANDATORY DISCLOSURES (FED. R. CIV. P. 26(A)(1))

Advise the court whether the parties have stipulated to a different method of disclosure than is required by Fed. R. Civ. P. 26(a)(1) or have agreed not to require any Rule 26(a)(1) disclosures.

ELECTRONIC INFORMATION DISCLOSURES (FED. R. CIV. P. 26(F))

The parties should provide (a) a brief description of their proposals regarding the disclosure or discovery of electronically stored information (and/or attach a proposed order) and/or (b) identify any disputes regarding the same.

STIPULATION REGARDING CLAIMS OF PRIVILEGE/PROTECTION OF TRIAL PREPARATION MATERIALS (FED. R. CIV. P. 26(F))

The parties should provide a brief description of the provisions of any proposed order governing claims of privilege or of protection as trial preparation material after production (and/or attach a proposed order).

COMPLETION OF DISCOVERY:

(1) Date all discovery complete [approximately 60 days prior to trial date according to Track] (2) If there are issues for early discovery, date for completion of discovery on those issues.

INTERROGATORIES:

A maximum of (number) [presumptive limit 25] interrogatories by each party to any other party. Responses due 30 days after service unless otherwise agreed to pursuant to Fed. R. Civ. P. 29.

REQUESTS FOR ADMISSION:

A maximum of *(number)* requests for admission by each party to any other party. Responses due 30 days after service unless otherwise agreed to pursuant to Fed. R. Civ. P. 29.

DEPOSITIONS:

A maximum of *(number)* [presumptive limit 10] depositions by plaintiff(s) and *(number)* [presumptive limit 10] by defendant(s).

Each deposition (other than of /name\) limited to a maximum of *(number)* [Presumptive Limit 7] hours unless extended by agreement of the parties.

DATES OF DISCLOSURE OF EXPERTS AND EXPERTS' WRITTEN REPORTS AND SUPPLEMENTATIONS:

Plaintiff:
due date

Defendant:
due date

Supplementations under Rule 26(e) due time(s) or interval(s).

Advise the court whether the parties have stipulated to a different form of expert report than that specified in Fed. R. Civ. P. 26(a)(2).

CHALLENGES TO EXPERT TESTIMONY:

due date: [no later than 45 days prior to trial]

OTHER ITEMS

JOINDER OF ADDITIONAL PARTIES:

Plaintiff:
due date

Defendant:
due date

THIRD-PARTY ACTIONS:
due date

AMENDMENT OF PLEADINGS:

Plaintiff:
due date

Defendant:
due date

DISPOSITIVE MOTIONS:

To Dismiss:
due date [no later than 90 days after preliminary pretrial]

For Summary Judgment:
due date [no later than 120 days prior to trial date according to Track]

SETTLEMENT POSSIBILITIES:

1. is likely

2. is unlikely

3. cannot be evaluated prior to (date)

4. may be enhanced by ADR:

    a. Request to the court

    b. Outside source

Joint Statement Re Mediation:

The parties shall indicate a date by which mediation, if any, will occur.

Witnesses and Exhibits:

[No dates necessary; due dates—10 days before final pretrial conference but not less than 30 days before trial for lists (included in final pretrial statements) and 14 days after service of final pretrial statement for objections—set by clerk's notice of trial assignment.]

Trial Estimate:

number of days

Trial Date:

The parties shall set out an agreed trial date—adhering to time periods as mandated by the chosen track assignment—using a preset jury selection day as provided on the court's web site (www.nhd.uscourts.gov). If the parties cannot agree on a date, they shall set out their respective proposed dates.

Preliminary Pretrial Conference:

The parties [request] [do not request] a preliminary pretrial conference with the court before entry of the scheduling order. [NOTE: The parties should plan to attend the preliminary pretrial conference as scheduled unless otherwise notified by the court.]

Other Matters:

The parties should list here their positions on any other matters which should be brought to the court's attention including other orders that should be entered under Fed. R. Civ. P. 26(c) or 16(b) and (c).

The state courts, through the Conference of Chief Justices, have also been proactive in dealing with e-discovery issues. The Conference of Chief Justices has adopted guidelines similar to the practices in federal court for state courts to use in considering issues related to e-discovery. Those guidelines can be obtained from the National Center for State Courts' website, which is www.ncsconline.org.

Finally, the paralegal, lawyer, and client must work closely to deal with issues relating to the search, maintenance, and retrieval of ESI and avoid costly sanctions and adverse judgments that are likely for failure to follow proper protocol for ESI. Both Rule 37 and, increasingly, civil actions for spoliation of evidence are used to compensate for the loss of important evidence. In *Zubulake v. UBS Warburg LLC,*[6] the landmark case for e-discovery production and cost sharing criteria, a former employee was ultimately awarded a $29 million verdict on her discrimination claim. After many disputes regarding the production of ESI, at trial the court gave a jury instruction on spoliation, directing jurors to presume that certain e-mails that the defendant never produced would have contained information detrimental to the defendant. Also in *U.S. v. Philip Morris,*[7] the court imposed nearly $3 million in sanctions against Philip Morris for e-discovery violations. As an additional sanction, the court also precluded Phillip Morris from calling certain witnesses in its defense. District court actions for spoliation of evidence claims exist in many states, including California, Pennsylvania, and New Jersey.[8]

In conclusion, the burdens on attorneys to counsel clients and paralegals to become familiar with their business and ESI practices have increased. Attorneys and paralegals must be knowledgeable about information systems so that information can be disclosed and effectively organized and retrieved. Paralegals, attorneys, and clients must work together to practice preventive law. In good faith, attorneys and the paralegals who work with them must help clients develop standard procedures, consistent with sound business practices, for retaining and purging information and recycling media; develop systems to segregate privileged and confidential information; and develop a comprehensive plan to educate the client's employees on their responsibilities in the use, destruction, and storage of electronic information.

Q: What can paralegals expect when working with outside ESI providers?

A: Answers provided by James K. Wagner, CEO and Co-Founder of DiscoverReady, LLC, a national provider of discovery management and document review services to Fortune 500 legal departments.

Throughout the course of our work, our project managers and attorneys frequently work alongside paralegals, litigation support professionals, and inside counsel attorneys on the corporate side. Our work is always supervised and signed off on by the outside counsel law firm, to ensure that our efforts properly support and dovetail with the legal service providers assigned to each matter. Costs for our e-mail review projects range from a few thousand dollars to millions. The cost is determined by a number of factors, including how many e-mail custodians the matter includes, the aggressiveness of the project's timeline, and the degree to which our resources are tapped

---

6. 229 F.R.D. 422 (S.D.N.Y. 2004).

7. 327 F. Supp. 2d 21 (D.C. Dist. 2004).

8. 19 COA 2d 249 (2008).

for the project. DiscoverReady assesses project cost by setting a fixed price per document, so budgets can be accurately set for each project.

Q: What are the litigation paralegal's roles in working with outside ESI providers?

A: Paralegals are essential to the success of our projects, since they do both substantive work and project coordination . . . . The paralegals that we work with regularly perform project management roles, as well as managing much of the technical litigation support process. They oversee document collections and preparation of exhibits and trial binders. Out of all legal professionals, paralegals are generally the best trained in how to use the technology. They supervise the technical specifications of the litigation databases that we use to complete our review projects.

Q: How can paralegals best work with outside ESI providers?

A: The best paralegals provide a level of professional planning and project management that is critically important to the successful execution of any discovery review. When paralegals understand the significance and value of a good plan and they proactively manage that plan's components, there is a much greater chance of overall project success . . . . Ideally, paralegals will take the time to prepare a formal project plan and to document and track the decision-making and execution process. It helps if they have a strong handle on the database and technology that we will need to access to execute our part of the project . . . . Paralegals must be organized, recognizing that they need to have a plan from the outset of our work together. They need to stay on top of things and ensure that there's a logical, defensible process in place from beginning to end. Their jobs require both assertiveness and diplomacy, and they need to enlist the cooperation of others in what they are doing. Paralegals have a difficult balancing act to perform. The relationship between paralegals, their clients, and their outside litigation support providers must be a "give and take" relationship. Each party has the ability to make the other look very good . . . . or very bad. Paralegals need to take the time to teach their outsourcing providers about what they do and how their firm needs things done. They should also invest time to understand the processes and needs of their providers so there are no unwelcome surprises.

TABLE 7.1: PERSPECTIVES FOR THE ATTORNEY-PARALEGAL TEAM

While your attorney is working on	You might assist by . . . .
• Deciding on the technological and organizational solutions to use in e-discovery	• Drafting a key IT person/keeper of the records discovery request to cover sources of information sought and expenses of retrieval • Selecting key search and concept search terms • Making an organizational chart and information technology chart for both key personnel and likely sources of information for both clients and adversaries • Drafting discovery requests in connection with e-discovery issues
• Conducting e-discovery and responding to e-discovery requests	• Coordinating with client through search for responsive material • Determining sources of stored material likely to have responsive information and estimating costs of retrieval • Assembling responsive material, drafting objections to requests, and drafting privilege log • Reviewing opponents' compliance, responses, and deficiencies • Addressing ongoing discovery and compliance issues as most local rules require • Drafting letters and Rule 37 sanction requests regarding discovery deficiencies

• Complying with the rules on e-discovery	• Finalizing draft of privilege log with the attorney
	• Reviewing with clients discovery requests, search efforts, responses, and likely problems with disagreements regarding compliance
	• Establishing a comfort level that the search complies with discovery requests and that final responses accurately reflect the matter

KEY TERMS

attachments	harvesting
backup	initial disclosures
compliance conferencing	IT specialist
computer forensics specialist	key concept searches
computer network	key term searches
data filtering	legal hold
deleted files	metadata
discovery compliance and privilege	native file format
discovery sources	optical character recognition
e-discovery	Outlook
e-discovery plans	portable document format
e-discovery retrieval	privilege log
e-discovery searches	PST file format
electronically stored information (ESI)	sampling
	sanctions
e-mail string	search methodology
file server	Spoliation of Evidence
fuzzy searches	TIFF

DISCUSSION QUESTIONS

1. What are some of the key terms, programs, software, and technological advances dealing with ESI that paralegals must be familiar with?

2. What are the paralegal's roles in effectively and efficiently assisting the attorney with ESI matters?

3. What are some best practices that paralegals should employ when dealing with ESI?

4. What are some key tips to keep in mind regarding compliance with the rules on e-discovery?

5. Refer back to *Woodward v. WelcomeMart:*

   a. Draft a sample e-discovery request on behalf of the Woodwards that asks WelcomeMart to turn over any internal company e-mails and any other electronic information on WelcomeMart's computers.

8

Assisting with Testimonial Evidence

From coordinating witnesses to digesting depositions, this chapter covers the essentials of a paralegal's role in assisting with testimonial evidence and getting the client or witnesses ready for testimony.

Chapter Overview

By the end of this chapter, you will be familiar with

- the paralegal's role in witness preparation;

- coordinating witnesses and their statements;

- taking a witness statement;

- assisting with depositions;

- digesting depositions;

- assisting with witness presentation at trial.

Testimonial evidence is a very important part of the attorney's presentation at trial—and the paralegal can play an important role in coordinating, obtaining, maintaining, and safekeeping testimonial evidence.

The Paralegal's Role in Witness Preparation

The paralegal has several functions when it comes to preparing witnesses for trial. The paralegal may be in charge of coordinating witnesses and their statements. The paralegal may also assist the attorney with interviewing witnesses (which was discussed in Chapter 5) and locating witnesses. Furthermore, the paralegal may assist with depositions, from scheduling and coordination to deposition digests. At times, the paralegal serves the function of "hand-holder": she is in charge of ensuring that the witness is comfortable, confident, and ready to testify.

Most importantly, paralegals must understand what information is necessary to cull from each witness's statement—whether it is obvious information that the witness has shared or information the paralegal sees between the lines. An essential part of the paralegal's function is to let the attorney know what to look for in each witness's testimony as well as to keep the attorney updated on witness information.

TAKING A WITNESS STATEMENT

The paralegal may assist the attorney with locating witnesses, coordinating and scheduling witnesses, and obtaining information from witnesses. There are several ways to take a witness statement: a witness may make a handwritten or typed statement, a recorded statement, or a statement in response to a written questionnaire. Your attorney may also ask you to draft the statement in the form of an affidavit—a sworn statement made under oath in which the affiant swears that the contents of the statement are true. When reducing the witness's statement to an affidavit, the witness should date and sign the statement under the pains and penalties of perjury. Before signing, the witness must read the statement carefully for content, accuracy, and completeness.

Always carefully coordinate the taking of a witness's statement with your attorney. The attorney may want to ensure that some specific points previously discussed are contained in a witness's written statement, or the attorney may not want a written statement if the witness's statement is unfavorable.

FIGURE 8.1: SAMPLE AFFIDAVIT

AFFIDAVIT OF MIMI WOODWARD

I, MIMI WOODWARD, being duly sworn state the following is true based upon my own personal knowledge:

1. My name is Mimi Woodward. I am the sister of Christopher Woodward.

2. On June 11, 2008, I was in the WelcomeMart store located at 131 Boulevard in Nita City, Nita.

3. I was at the WelcomeMart store with my brother, Christopher Woodward, who was attempting to pick up his prescription medication.

4. While in the store looking for some things, I was accosted by the store's security guard, Bart Harayda, who took me and my brother Christopher into a small room in the front of the store.

5. Bart Harayda locked the door of the room behind us and did not let me or my brother Christopher leave.

6. I did not give Bart Harayda consent to take me into the room.

7. Since Harayda forcibly took me into that room I missed ten days of work as a restaurant manager due to anxiety and panic attacks about this incident.

8. Since Harayda forcibly took me into that room, I have experienced panic attacks and been treated for anxiety by Dr. Sophia Caroline, a psychologist practicing in Nita City.

9. Since that day I continue to suffer from night sweats on a regular basis.

I certify that the above statements are true. I sign this affidavit under the pains and penalties of perjury.

_____ Dated: _____

MIMI WOODWARD

ASSISTING WITH DEPOSITIONS

Depositions can be the source of some of the most important pieces of evidence in a case. In addition to fact investigation, information gathering, and verification, a deposition can serve the purpose of fact preservation: for example, a witness may become unavailable to testify at trial, and the deposition may be used in place of testimony. Plus, depending on how a deposition goes, either or both sides may be influenced regarding the strength and value of the case for settlement, so depositions can be used to evaluate settlement and trial options as well.

Preparing for a Deposition

Paralegals can be invaluable in helping the attorney prepare for a deposition. First, paralegals must be clear about the types of information the attorney is trying to elicit from the deponent—for instance, is the attorney looking for new information from a crucial witness, looking to preserve the witness's testimony, or looking for information to support a theory in the case? Investigate (and brief your attorney on) how the deponent and the deposition fit into the client's story—for example, is the witness's testimony likely to support or undercut the client's version of the events? By better understanding the purpose of the deposition and the likely purpose of the deponent's story, you and your attorney will be better able to come up with the right questions and information to elicit from the deponent.

Paralegals can also relay important information about witnesses and their testimony to the attorney. For example, if you discover that the witness is likely to become unavailable to testify at trial (because the witness is seriously ill, likely to move, or elderly), then you need to let your attorney know, so that he can better strategize about conducting the deposition, preserving the testimony, and asking the right kinds of questions. You may be asked to brief the attorney in writing or orally about the witness and how the witness and the deposition fit into the case overall. You may also be asked to monitor the witness and update the attorney periodically about the witness. Before the deposition, read through all of the documents that give you some background on the deponent, including prior witness statements and any records you have obtained through your investigation and fact gathering. Using those prior documents and records, also try to figure out where potential problems may arise with the witness's testimony at the deposition.

You can also assist the attorney with putting together a checklist of "must-have" pieces of information that need to be discovered or presented at the deposition. For example, if you are dealing with a favorable witness, you will want to make sure the attorney asks all questions necessary to obtain favorable information during the deposition. Conversely, if you are dealing with an adverse witness, your attorney will likely want to focus on asking comprehensive questions about those parts of the deponent's story that do not add up.

Before the deposition, you should familiarize yourself with all the documents and records that your attorney may need during the deposition. If you are present at the deposition, part of your role may be to filter the documents your attorney needs as the attorney is asking questions, and to direct and focus the attorney's attention on the information that needs to be elicited from the witness. To be able to do that, you will have to know the documents and the purpose of the deposition very well.

If applicable, paralegals can also assist the attorney with checklists for conducting the deposition (such as the kinds of questions to ask, documents that need a foundation, and information to obtain). If you are in charge of case management, you may also assist the attorney with drafting questions for the deponent—remember that questions should be precise, short, plain, and simple.

Finally, paralegals assist with coordinating scheduling for the deposition. You may be in charge of sending a deposition notice to the deponent, along with serving any required subpoenas; you may also be in charge of scheduling a transcriptionist to take down the record of the deposition.

CHECKLIST 8.1: PREPARING FOR A DEPOSITION

- Check with your attorney about the purpose and focus of the deposition.
- Understand the purpose of the deposition.
- Relay important information about witnesses and their testimony to the attorney.

- Put together a checklist of "must-have" pieces of information that need to be discovered at the deposition.

- Be familiar with all the documents and records that your attorney may need during the deposition.

- Assist the attorney with checklists for conducting the deposition.

- Coordinate scheduling for the deposition.

Digesting Depositions

After the deposition is conducted, the deponent's testimony is transcribed into a deposition transcript. These transcripts can be hundreds of pages long—so most attorneys will want a digest, or short summary, of a deposition transcript to use in the case. Often, the paralegal is entrusted with digesting the deposition or obtaining a digest from an outside provider.

Check with your attorney about the kinds of pertinent information the attorney wants you to put into the deposition digest. One of the paralegal's functions is to cull the essential information from the deposition and determine how the deponent's statements fit into the case. Also determine whether your attorney wants to use a paper or electronic digest, or both.

Determine what types of indexes the attorney wants you to obtain—for example, do you need to create your own word index, order a specialized Min-u-Script, or do both? Are you cross-indexing deposition digests? For example, are you indexing digests by date as well as reference to a specific event or word? Determine how your attorney wants to set up the index system that will accompany your deposition digests in the case. Remember that your role here is to achieve maximum efficiency and let the attorney find information as quickly and effectively as possible.

When digesting the deposition, be sure the deposition digest includes proper page and line references. Once the digest is complete, input the information into all relevant databases, whether electronic or paper.

Checklist 8.2: Digesting Depositions

- Determine the kinds of pertinent information the attorney wants you to put into the deposition digest.

- Determine whether your attorney wants to use a paper or electronic digest, or both, as well as what types of indexes the attorney wants you to obtain.

- Input the information into all relevant databases, whether electronic or paper.

FIGURE 8.2: SAMPLE DEPOSITION TRANSCRIPT EXCERPT

After being sworn, the witness was questioned by Attorney Better as follows:

1   Q.   Please state your name.

2   A.   My name is Christopher Woodward.

3   Q.   Where do you reside?

4   A.   I live at 1 Main Street here in Nita.

5   Q.   What is your national origin?

6   A.   I am African-American.

7   Q.   What happened on June 11, 2008?

8   A.   I had come from having surgery on my mouth that morn-
9   ing so I went to get a prescription filled at WelcomeMart.

10   Q.   What time was your surgery that morning?

11   A.   My surgery was at 7:00 a.m. and it was over fairly quickly.

12   Q.   Where did you go after the surgery was finished?

13   A.   The WelcomeMart near the doctor's office is on Federal
14   Street.

15   Q.   Why did you go to that WelcomeMart?

16   A.   I was in pain so I wanted to get the pills as quickly as
17   possible.

18   Q.   How did you get to that WelcomeMart?

19   A.   Well, I couldn't drive because of the anesthesia so my sister
20   Mimi drove me there and back.

21   Q.   What happened when you got to the WelcomeMart?

22   A.   Well, I went into the store to get the prescription filled
23   while Mimi was parking the car.

Page 1

Deposition of Christopher Woodward

ASSISTING WITH THE PRESENTATION OF WITNESSES AT TRIAL

Today's sound-bite society has a short attention span. In this new information age where time is measured in nanoseconds, lawyers and paralegals who are planning the trial strategy for a case must plan to use it wisely.

Attorneys plan the presentation of their witnesses so that the testimony will have the greatest impact—in some instances, however, the least effect may be desirable, as in the case of the testimony of a necessary but weak witness. Jurors are most alert at the beginning and end of a case, at the beginning and end of the day, at the beginning and end of each witness's testimony, and when they first come back from a break. When preparing questions for testifying witnesses, remember that jurors at some point get hungry and lose interest in what is said; shortly after returning from lunch, they may get tired or grow bored with the presentations. Plan the presentation of your witnesses and the evidence—both good and bad—with an understanding of these facts. When you are assisting your attorney with questions for the witnesses, keep the testimony of each witness brief, and that will help ensure that jurors pay attention to the information elicited. Always remember that attorneys seek to elicit important information when the jurors are most alert.

Paralegals may assist with testimonial evidence at trial in various ways:

- The paralegal may help arrange the order of witnesses at trial and may be in charge of scheduling and coordinating each witness's appearance;

- The paralegal may be entrusted with making sure that each witness appears at her scheduled time—this may entail checking up on the witness, assisting the witness with travel and transportation arrangements, or even picking the witness up on the day of her testimony;

- The paralegal may serve the function of "hand-holder" when it comes to witnesses: the paralegal may sit with the witnesses outside the courtroom, making sure the witness is comfortable and confident with testifying; making sure the witness keeps focused on the information that the witness will relay during her testimony; keeping the witness aware of what will go on during testimony; and making sure that nerves will not get the best of the witness;

- The paralegal may help the attorney coordinate the use of exhibits and documents during witness testimony;

- The paralegal may assist the attorney with creating checklists of essential information that the attorney wants to ask during the witness's testimony;

- The paralegal may be asked to watch for and alert the attorney to testimony that contradicts the witness's earlier statements—for example, those made at a prior deposition—and then locate that inconsistent testimony in the prior deposition.

TABLE 8.1: PERSPECTIVES FOR THE ATTORNEY-PARALEGAL TEAM

While your attorney is working on	You might assist by . . . .
• Preparing the client or witness for trial	• Taking care of scheduling, transportation, and accomodations • Assisting the attorney with drafting questions • Coordinating all supporting documents that the attorney will need in questioning and preparing the witness
• Reviewing deposition testimony	• Digesting depositions and key documents • Locating witnesses referred to in the deposition and documents
• Ensuring that the witness is ready to testify	• Interfacing with the witness • Increasing the witness's level of comfort • Acting as the person of contact

KEY TERMS	
affidavit	index
cross-index	testimonial evidence
deponent	transcript
deposition	witness statement
deposition digest	

DISCUSSION QUESTIONS

1. What personal and professional skills do paralegals need in order to effectively assist attorneys with testimonial evidence?

2. Refer back to the case of *Woodward v. WelcomeMart.*

   a. Who are some key witnesses that Patty, the paralegal for the plaintiffs should interview? What types of information should she elicit and seek to include in a witness statement?

   b. Who are some key witnesses that Danny, the paralegal for the defendant, should interview? What types of information should he elicit and seek to include in a witness statement?

3. Patty's attorney has just deposed the doctor who treated Christopher Woodward for his injuries after the incident at WelcomeMart.

   a. What purposes do you think the doctor's deposition served?

   b. What questions do you think the attorney asked?

   c. What information do you think Patty might include in the deposition digest?

EXHIBIT PREPARATION, MAINTENANCE, AND COORDINATION

Paralegals are often trusted with tangible and demonstrative evidence preparation, organization, and maintenance, and this chapter describes related tasks.

CHAPTER OVERVIEW

By the end of this chapter, you should be familiar with

- exhibit preparation;
- factors to consider when preparing exhibits;
- exhibit maintenance and coordination;
- working with outside providers on exhibits.

While testimonial evidence is important at trial, sometimes it takes more than just the spoken word of witnesses to convince the jury to rule for your client. Attorneys often use tangible or demonstrative exhibits to show jurors a key fact and enhance the presentation at trial. For example, exhibits—such as the sample x-ray and prescription included at the end of this chapter—can help establish the plaintiff's damages in a personal injury case.

THE PARALEGAL'S ROLES IN EXHIBIT PREPARATION AND MAINTENANCE

Paralegals play four key roles in preparing, coordinating, and maintaining exhibits: they perform legwork research to get the exhibits prepared; ensure that the exhibits meet the attorney's specifications; ensure that the exhibits are affordable and within the resources allotted; and ensure that the exhibits are prepared, assembled, and in working order when needed at the trial.

Obtaining and Preparing Exhibits

If you are asked to assist with exhibits, you will first have to consult with your attorney to decide what exactly you will need to obtain. You must figure out what type of exhibits will best demonstrate the client's case to the jury. There are many options to consider for displaying exhibits. For example, will an oversized poster board do the trick, or does your attorney want individual copies of an exhibit passed out to jurors? Do you need to show a video deposition in the courtroom on a large screen or monitor, or will you display a presentation from a laptop and projection, or use a simple overhead projector? Do you want to hire an outside provider to work the equipment in the courtroom, or can someone from the firm take care of that? Do you need to re-create an object through the use of models or a replica—a model car, for example, or even a skeleton? To decide, you will have to consult your attorney for his "vision" of presenting the client's side of the story, and then decide what the attorney would like to use to present that story.

The paralegal must get a sense of the attorney's purposes for each exhibit—this will help you ensure that you obtain the right types of exhibits for the right reasons. For example, if your attorney asks you to get an oversized poster board depicting the location of the accident scene, ask how the attorney intends to use the board at trial. If witnesses will write on the board consecutively, it may make sense to obtain a laminated board that can be erased; conversely, if the idea is to preserve each witness's diagram of the events, it will make sense to obtain extra copies of the board in a finish that cannot be erased.

Next, discuss your technology options. It won't do you any good to decide that you'd like to present something to the jury on a large screen if your courtroom doesn't allow for that kind of presentation. Find out in advance what technology the courtroom has built in and what equipment you'll have to bring to make that technology work. (*See* Chapter Ten for an explanation of trial technologies available.)

Think about your time frame. Typically, the earlier you get exhibits ready, the better. When deciding on the kinds of exhibits you'd like to use, factor in the time it will take to get them prepared. A simple enlargement and mounting to a poster board of an image can be ready in as little as twenty-four hours, while a PowerPoint presentation that has many images and needs to be carefully put together may take days or weeks to get right.

Finally, keep resources in mind. Whether you have an unlimited budget or limited resources, your attorney will have to make use of the funds available in the best way possible to make information contained in the exhibits come to life. A small budget trial presentation may consist of a few 2' by 3' or 3' by 4' poster boards at $100 each, while state-of-the-art, elaborate video with presentation DVD display systems could add tens of thousands of dollars to your budget.

Working with Outside Providers

It is rare nowadays for a paralegal or other member of the firm's staff to prepare exhibits in-house. Instead, most attorneys will outsource exhibit preparation to outside providers, whether it's the local copy shop or a national chain of litigation support providers that specializes in the specific type of exhibit preparation your attorney needs. Outside providers can offer law firms and paralegals a host of different services, ranging from document reproduction to exhibit preparation to trial graphics.

Most likely, it will be the paralegal's job to coordinate exhibit preparation with outside providers. So you'll have to work well together with providers and establish long-lasting relationships with people you can call on to have that important exhibit made—sometimes at the last minute!

Before signing on with a provider for a case, get references, preferably from other lawyers and firms that have used the provider successfully in the past. If you pick an irresponsible provider for a project, it will be your reputation (and maybe your job) on the line if the provider fails to come through. Put together a list of outside providers that you can call on, noting their prices, specialties, locations, and typical time frame required to get the job done.

At some point, it may also be a good idea to put together a list of recurring items (such as laptops, projectors, or screens) that your firm owns, which will not have to be rented from an outside provider. Keep the list in an accessible space where people can reserve them check off items as they take them outside the firm and bring them back. Don't forget to update as necessary.

In each order that you place with an outside provider, specify exactly what your attorney wants. Be as clear in writing as possible about your attorney's instructions, whether they deal with dimensions, colors, or language.

CHECKLIST 9.1: OBTAINING AND PREPARING EXHIBITS

- Consult with the attorney to determine what type of exhibits best demonstrate your client's case.

- Understand the attorney's purpose for each exhibit.

- Discuss your technology options.

- Keep your time frame and resources in mind when planning for exhibits.

- Establish long-lasting relationships with outside providers you can call on.

- Before signing on with a provider for a case, get references.

- When working with an outside provider, specify exactly what your attorney wants and be as clear as possible in relaying the attorney's instructions to the provider.

VERIFYING, COORDINATING, AND MAINTAINING EXHIBITS

Next, you'll need to check the exhibits to ensure that the exhibits arrive in the condition and according to the specifications that were relayed to you by your attorney. It goes without saying that you have to double-check all of your exhibits when they come in from the outside provider for accuracy, substance, content, and presentation.

You must also ensure that all exhibits comport with relevant rules of evidence and admissibility. Also, ensure that the exhibits do what they are supposed to do: help persuade and convince the jury to find for your client. Paralegals shouldn't just be functionaries when it comes to exhibit preparation—they should think about the substance of the exhibits to make sure the exhibits are clear and persuasive. A paralegal's perspective may greatly help the attorney create convincing exhibits: the people on the jury didn't go to law school, and neither did the paralegal; it may be helpful to have the perspective of a person who doesn't have "law school blinders" on!

Undoubtedly, even if you relayed your attorney's specifications to the outside provider perfectly, something could go wrong in the end—a blown-up picture may look too blurry, for example, or an e-mailed description may use the wrong font and appear out-of-place. Always double-check all exhibits that were entrusted to your care before forwarding them for your attorney's approval—and never, never bring an exhibit to the trial before checking to be sure that it is exactly what your attorney wanted to present to the jury.

Check with the provider ahead of time as to whether the exhibits require any special care or storage, and if so, make provisions for that care or storage in advance, before you get the exhibits back. As with any important documents in the case, exhibits should be properly indexed and cross-indexed, and stored in a secure and organized manner. Decide in advance who will be in charge of exhibit coordination and maintenance. If this is you, then you're entrusted to know where the exhibits are at all times. Determine how the exhibits will be transported to the courtroom—oversized exhibits will need an oversized case to get there undamaged, for example.

CHECKLIST 9.2: VERIFYING, COORDINATING, AND MAINTAINING EXHIBITS

- Double-check exhibits for accuracy, substance, content, and presentation.
- Ensure that all exhibits comport with relevant rules of evidence and admissibility.
- Check with the provider for any special handling instructions and make provisions accordingly.

- Index and cross-index all exhibits.
- Know where the exhibits are at all times.
- Determine how the exhibits will be transported to the courtroom.

Ensuring That the Exhibits Are Ready to Go

Finally, you will likely be entrusted with ensuring that the exhibits are prepared, assembled, and in working order when they are needed by your attorney at the trial. If you are using technology with your trial presentation, then always, always, always triple-check to make sure the technology is fully functional on the day that it will be used to enhance your attorney's presentation. It does not get much worse than a presentation with poorly functioning technology.

This means you'll have to make sure that all equipment and technology your attorney needs to present the exhibits will be in the courtroom well before your attorney needs it. Chalkboards and tripods can disappear from courtrooms in the matter of weeks, days, or even hours—so don't count on the equipment being there just because you saw it there previously. For anything that will be presented electronically, make sure you have a back-up plan for when the hard disk crashes or the computer file disappears. As with documents, there should be some level of redundancy and cross-indexing with exhibits to ensure you can turn to a hard-copy version if the electronic version fails to go well.

Make sure that you have assembled all of the key documents your attorney will need at trial when presenting an exhibit to the jury. Also make sure that all the witnesses who are needed to support the information on the exhibit are able and ready to testify.

Bring extras! Whether it's a power strip, tripod, or back-up of that laptop presentation, it's better to have an extra ready to go than to be without a key exhibit your attorney needed to show the jury desperately.

If you're working on location, be sure you give yourself extra time to get exhibits set up and ready to go. You need to do the same amount of careful planning on location as you would if you were presenting the exhibits at a trial in the courthouse next door—perhaps more, if you are unfamiliar with the place. Again, research and contract with outside providers as early as possible, get references, and give yourself some time to verify and double-check exhibits before handing them over to your attorney.

CHECKLIST 9.3: ENSURING THAT THE EXHIBITS ARE READY TO GO

- The final step to exhibit preparation and maintenance occurs right outside the courtroom: you must make sure that the exhibits are ready to be presented at the precise time that your attorney needs to use them.

- Ensure that all key documents and exhibits are properly assembled and all witnesses needed to support them are able and ready to testify.

- Bring extras and have a back-up plan!

- Give yourself extra time to get exhibits set up and ready to go.

SAMPLE EXHIBIT 1: A SAMPLE PHOTOGRAPH DEPICTING THE INTERSECTION WHERE AN ACCIDENT OCCURRED

SAMPLE EXHIBIT 2: A SAMPLE X-RAY

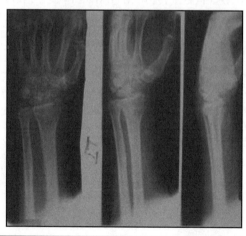

SAMPLE EXHIBIT 3: DR. BHASIN'S PRESCRIPTION FOR CHRISTOPHER WOODWARD

BHASIN SURGICAL ASSOCIATES

500 Federal Street
City of Nita, Nita State

Name Christopher Woodward   **Date** June 11, 2008

Address 3 Hickory Hill   **Age/Wt** 31/250
City of Nita, Nita State

Rx Oxycontin 800 mg
Disp #10
Sig: Take 1 capsule every four hours as
needed for pain

Penicillin 250 mg
Disp #21
Sig: Take 1 every 8 hours

/s/ Dr. R. Bhasin

Dispense as Written   **Substitution Permissible**

Refills   1

Q: How can paralegals best assist outside providers with projects?

A. Answer by Thomas Perry, National Sales Manager, Williams Lea, Inc., a national company that provides e-discovery services, reprographics, imaging, and digital processing services to law firms and attorneys.

Paralegals can assist [outside providers] by taking the time to understand the services [they] offer before the "Big Job" hits. Discussing the purpose of large or unique projects helps as well so we can act in a consultative manner. This will allow [outside providers] to tailor the work done to the specific requirements and avoid wasted time.

In more specific detail, it helps when paralegals:

- Know what program will be used to view the digital files they're requesting;

- Offer acceptable abbreviations for filenames for legal documents;

- Indicate what form final delivery should take, especially if there are multiple, equally common options;

- Know the common file types with which they work;

- Inform us as soon as possible of incoming work or changes to an existing job, even if the details are still unknown;

- Explain what legal issues, if any, are involved with a particular job: [authentication] tracking, exact reproduction of images (rather than de-skewing/de-speckling for easier reading), redaction requirements, etc.

Maintain an active dialogue with [outside providers] even when a job is not on the table. This lets [outside providers] keep the paralegal informed of new technology and recent trends . . . . Act as a good communication buffer between [outside providers] and the attorneys. Keep a flow of the dialogue.

TABLE 9.1: PERSPECTIVES FOR THE ATTORNEY-PARALEGAL TEAM

While your attorney is working on	You might assist by . . . .
• Deciding which documents and images to use at trial	• Getting documents and images assembled • Making arrangements with outside providers for preparing exhibits and demonstrative evidence

• Establishing a theme for presentation strategy and selecting the media that will be employed in the presentation of the case	• Ensuring that the attorney will be able to present the evidence according to plan (both from the standpoint of conducting legal research regarding evidence and the availability of the physical evidence) • Coordinating use of technology in the courtroom • Ensuring that all equipment and other tools needed to present the evidence are available at the time of trial
• Presenting exhibits and demonstrative evidence during the trial	• Locating documents and other things as the attorney needs them • Ensuring that all exhibits are in place • Ensuring that all technology and trial tools are working • Coordinating exhibits and documents to ensure the attorney has access to all exhibits and documents as she needs

KEY TERMS	
demonstrative evidence	outside providers
evidence	outsourcing exhibit preparation
exhibit	replica
maintaining exhibits	video deposition

DISCUSSION QUESTIONS

1. Your attorney has asked you to prepare an oversized poster board depicting the plaintiff's injuries in the case of a client who suffered physical and mental injuries that occurred during a serious car accident. The plaintiff broke his right arm and was hospitalized for two days due to complications from surgery. Since the plaintiff was a laborer, he was unable to return to his construction job until two months had passed and he had completed a course of physical therapy. Put together a checklist for tackling this project. What considerations will you have to pay attention to?

2. What challenges might arise in exhibit preparation, coordination, and maintenance? How can those challenges be overcome through careful planning?

3. Refer back to the case of *Woodward v. WelcomeMart.*

   a. What exhibits might be presented by both sides?

   b. What roles may paralegals Patty and Danny play in obtaining, preparing, and coordinating those exhibits?

MASTERING TRIAL TECHNOLOGY

Paralegals must understand and make effective use of technology—inside and outside of the courtroom. This chapter introduces the basic technological tools and software used during and in preparation for trial. It also offers tips for mastering the technical side of trials and using technology to advance advocates' presentation of their materials.

CHAPTER OVERVIEW

By the end of this chapter, you will be familiar with

- various types of software and technology used to prepare for trial;
- trial technology in the courtroom;
- best practices in using litigation software and trial technology;
- the skills and knowledge necessary to manage litigation software and the technical side of trials and trial preparation;
- the paralegal's role in using litigation software and trial technology.

THE BASICS OF TRIAL TECHNOLOGY

Whether your team is trying to plan a high-tech trial on a low-tech budget or your office has unlimited resources and staff to assist your team with a dazzling electronic presentation at trial, it is still best to remember that while visual aids—such as exhibits displayed electronically, demonstrations, animations, and even PowerPoint presentations—are effective complements to the trial presentation, they should never dominate it. To be effective at trial, your team must get its message across to each jury member. Each juror learns in a variety of ways, so plan your presentation to take advantage of that fact. Jurors reward litigation teams who make things easier for them to understand.

Many lawyers still prefer displaying images and documents through the tried-and-true enlarged foam-core board exhibit on the classic tripod. Witnesses testifying under oath, who are subject to cross-examination, have provided audiences sufficient drama in the real world, in print, and on the stage and screen for centuries. The diagram of the intersection where the auto accident took place, the layout of the interior of the office building, and the time-line displayed on an oversized foam-core board are all examples of presentations that lend themselves better to old-school technology. Such items then serve as a center or anchor for the trial and can remain at the end of the jury box throughout the trial. The repetitive use of the anchor by counsel and witnesses provides jury members with essential and important information that they can then use to find for your client.

Today, technology is often a necessary part of courtroom presentation. A litigation team uses technology to enhance the jury's understanding of the issues—not simply to dazzle them. Jury studies show that much of the weight the jury gives to the message that your attorney is delivering comes from the manner of the delivery and visuals used. Words alone may fall on deaf ears.

In fact, we may fast be approaching the time when truly paperless trials are commonplace. Even now, e-mails, electronically stored information, spreadsheets, and other digital data form the bulk of our assembled discovery. The paper records that attorneys obtain are often scanned, stored into searchable databases, categorized electronically, and retrieved from a database with that same material. E-discovery issues often now dominate discovery, and the management of that information is a formidable task. Evidence, including documents, x-rays, photographs, deposition video, and demonstrative graphics loaded into litigation support software can be displayed colorfully and published to the jurors on larger-than-life TV screens. With basic annotation systems or "telestrators" like those used by analysts at sporting events, the attorney can easily direct the jury's attention to highlighted information. Emphasis can be supplied with color or other graphics during a witness's testimony or at closing, where it may be wise to use specific trial exhibits with important words highlighted.

To effectively assist your attorney, you must be aware of the technology that forms part of the trial attorney's basic arsenal. Every attorney and paralegal must be familiar with the basic operation of a laptop and a projector that can be attached to the laptop in order to display images on a large screen for the jury's viewing. In addition to the laptop and projector, an evidence presentation system may include an evidence or document camera to display evidence or other physical material; a network connecting the screens of the attorneys, clerk, judge, and witness together; and an illustration device. A DVD player capable of playing audio and video is a must if that media is not already reduced to digital format and stored in a computer system. Some courtrooms combine all of the controls for the technology into a single stand-alone unit, such as an integrated lectern/evidence presentation unit or a digital evidence presentation system that controls all video and digital displays in the courtroom.

Whatever technology your attorney chooses to use at trial, there are some things you must be familiar with in order to best assist your attorney.

The Skills and Knowledge You Need to Handle Litigation Software and Trial Technology

Paralegals must know how to select and operate the necessary hardware and software in use in today's courtrooms, so they can properly prepare and help their attorneys conduct technology-intensive trials or trials in which they must display visual or quantitative information. To that end, you must be familiar with the software and hardware used to organize cases and present visual information at trial. You will also need to be comfortable with the evidentiary rules involved in presenting evidence electronically or evidence that is electronic in nature.

Since many small law offices do not have the resources to invest large sums in the latest technology, it is important to understand basic legal strategies and low-cost technology options in the preparation and presentation of your case.

You must also remember that not all courtrooms are equipped with technological features that will support advanced presentations. The paralegal and attorney must consider this issue as the attorney decides what technology to employ in any given case. Some judges like new technology, while others favor the "good old days"—the latter's tolerance for miscues and delays that inevitably occur with the use of some technology must be carefully assessed.

Always bring backups, always bring everything you need to use that technology, and always plan for the worst to happen! This way, you will become the "go-to person" as problems arise. By planning for the best and anticipating the worst, you dramatically improve your team's chances for success.

Courtroom technology is always changing when it comes to both emerging technologies and physical resources available in a courtroom. Many federal courts are technologically friendly while most state courts, unfortunately, lag behind in technological advances—plan accordingly.

It is important that you get the basics down first. A good paralegal must be able to store and easily retrieve information in litigation support software, master the use of traditional database management and imaging software, learn how to take "soft-copy" information and display it to the jury with the use of a projector and a laptop, and use the resources available to support the attorney's efforts to present a persuasive case.

Since technology, and trial presentation technology specifically, is constantly changing, it is vital to recognize that your education does not stop when you finish your studies in a paralegal program—it has merely begun. The hard work comes when you enter the field. You must attend technology workshops and continuing education seminars, subscribe to online magazines and newsgroups that have the latest articles, look for ways to continue to educate yourself and your team on emerging technologies, and stay informed about cost-effective technological developments that will enhance your effectiveness.

A TECHNOLOGY PRIMER: LOOKING AT WHAT IS AVAILABLE

Depending on the amount of resources you have and your team's comfort level with technology, there are many other technological tools available to advance your team's presentation. Read on for a brief review of some of the technology that is used in litigation:

- **Animations and GCI Re-creations.** Models, demonstrations, and re-creations are three types of animations used to graphically demonstrate something. Models depict what something looks like; demonstrations show how something works; and re-creations reconstruct how an event likely took place. These 2D or 3D animations are valuable when explaining an accident, process, or other dynamic event. Animation videos visually take the jury into the heart of what is in issue in a case and display your version of the event or dispute in a fashion that is easy for the jury to understand.

- **Annotation Systems.** Annotation systems allow notes to be made directly on a digitally displayed document so that your team can circle, underline, or highlight areas of emphasis.

- **Barcode Readers.** These devices use the same technology that you see in the supermarket, and they allow for easy and quick access to information stored electronically. If the case is exhibit intensive, a barcode reader allows your team to make retrieval easier by simply swiping the previously scanned exhibit with the reader, thus making retrieval and display faster and simpler.

- **Digital Audio Recording Device.** This is a portable digital recording device that allows a user to record audio files into an MP3 or other digital format. A digital audio recording device records audio files and converts them to a digital format for ease of storage and retrieval.

- **Digital Presentation.** A digital presentation incorporates documents, text, graphics, digital images, clip art, and video on a display screen to visually deliver the message. A good example of a digital presentation is a PowerPoint presentation that incorporates multiple forms of media to convey the information.

- **Digital Projector.** A digital projector is a device that electronically projects information from a computer to a large display screen. Generally, the higher the pixel resolution that the projector has, the better the image that is displayed.

- **Demonstrative Board.** This is an enlarged exhibit on a large foam-core board used to display portions of the jury instructions, exhibits, graphs, charts, diagrams, and the like to the jury in a visually appealing way.

- **Digital Evidence Presentation System.** A digital evidence presentation system combines video and digital display technology to support all aspects of evidence presentation at trial. These units can be mobile or stationary and are used to control all video and digital displays in the courtroom.

- **Digital Slide Projector.** Digital slide projectors can be directly connected to a computer or used with a memory card loaded into the projector that will then display the selected image onto a screen.

- **Drivers.** Computers use drivers (software) that tell the computer how to use a piece of equipment, such as the driver for a printer. Windows and Mac operating software generally include the drivers necessary to use most projection devices. If that is not the case, the appropriate software will need to be loaded on the laptop or computer for the projector to display the images.

- **Digital Visual Interface.** DVI is a standard that defines the digital interface between digital devices, such as projectors and personal computers. For devices that support DVI, a digital-to-digital connection can be made, eliminating the conversion to analog and thereby displaying a superior image.

- **Electronic Case Filing.** With ECF, attorneys file pleadings and other documents electronically with courts through the Internet by using a standard Web browser. This can result in a completely electronic case file that does not have papers associated with it at the court. Therefore, all case information is available for examination during trial electronically through the Internet.

- **Enhanced Projection Systems.** These systems project a digital image onto a screen. Unlike with old-style projection systems, the image is continually displayed despite the attorney or the witness approaching the image and interrupting the light source.

- **Evidence or Document Cameras.** An evidence or document camera is used to display large images of physical evidence and material, such as photos, x-rays, DNA autoradiographs, transparencies, and 3-D objects onto a screen for ease of viewing and reference.

- **Handheld Computing Devices.** These handheld devices are often the mainstay of an attorney's management of her calendar and contacts. Also called personal digital assistants (PDAs), these devices are capable of storing vast amounts of information including e-mails, calendars, calculators, and databases. Blackberry, Palm, iPhone, PocketPC, and Handspring devices are all types of handheld computing devices in use by attorneys.

- **Laptop and Projector.** Most standard laptops display to the screen attached to the laptop and can be configured to externally project that image to a projector or monitor. Laptops let you switch displays among four different projection modes: laptop only, external monitor, digital projection only, and both laptop and external video projection. This switching is done by holding the function key (Fn) and hitting the appropriate key. This key typically either has a small icon that looks like a video screen or is labeled LCD. It is best to remember that photographs and video consume much of the laptop's resources, so always be sure that there is sufficient storage and RAM to quickly access this information.

- **Litigation Software.** These are database management programs that enable litigation teams to organize and store documents and other media, as well as support the team's trial preparation and presentation. Litigation software efficiently manages case information, including pleadings, documents, transcripts, and other media. It is very helpful for case analysis and trial presentation because it tracks, stores, and organizes all case materials so that they are fully searchable. The most widely used litigation software includes Summation, Concordance, Casemap, and Casesoft. A good paralegal would be familiar with each, although smaller firms often use Casesoft as their primary litigation support software. TrialMax is litigation software that also integrates documents, photographs, animations, deposition video, audio, and demonstrative graphics into a single trial preparation and presentation tool. E-beam and Sanction are also programs that provide litigation support.

- **Online Deposition Service.** This is a service enabling law firms to have secure online document repositories containing court documents, exhibits, transcripts, working papers, and any other case-specific documents. The system is used as a Web transcript repository to download transcripts of completed depositions and as an easy way to retrieve transcripts, exhibits, and schedules of past and upcoming depositions. Online depositions can also include the ability to conduct depositions online through videoconferencing equipment.

- **Overhead Projectors.** These devices allow images to be placed on the unit and displayed onto a screen. Images placed on clear plastic media, called transparencies, are used to display the image on a large screen. The light from the lamp travels through the transparency and up into a mirror, which displays it on a large screen.

- **Real-Time Transcription or Real-Time Reporting Equipment.** This technology delivers a transcript to the attorney's personal laptop computer as the speaker talks. Real-time transcription is the general term for transcription by stenographers and court reporters using computer-aided transcription technology to deliver text to computer screens within a few seconds of the speaker uttering the words. This specialized equipment and software allows the attorneys to make notes in the text and highlight portions for future reference.

- **Video Impeachment and Video Deposition Presentations.** These allow for retrieval and display of video depositions and video clips from a witness's prior video deposition, to be shown to the jury. A witness's prior video deposition can then be used to impeach that witness when he contradicts himself when testifying at trial. Knowing how to store, retrieve, and display video to a jury is vital because it is much easier to keep the jury's attention by playing video clips.

TABLE 10.1: PERSPECTIVES FOR THE ATTORNEY-PARALEGAL TEAM

While your attorney is working on	You might assist by . . . .
• Deciding what types of trial technology to use	• Being familiar and comfortable with using and accessing the technology the attorney chooses • Testing the technology and receiving training on it as needed • Ensuring that the technology chosen by the attorney is available and ready to use when needed • Planning for some level of redundancy to ensure that backups will be available on any technology that is being used • Making sure that the information needed is available in the format requested by the attorney

• Using litigation software	• Inputting information into databases • Becoming trained on and comfortable with the various features of the software, and at times coordinating training for others at the firm • Communicating with the provider regarding common mistakes and receiving additional training as necessary • Coordinating backups if necessary • Coordinating software updates for ease of use and ensuring that the software is kept up-to-date
• Using technology in the courtroom	• Making sure that all images and documents are properly loaded and easily accessible • Ensuring that backups are ready to use if a file is corrupted or lost • Pulling the hard copy of information that is being displayed as an exhibit • Pulling up files on the screen as your attorney presents to the jury • Taking advantage of technology to recap key evidence that was admitted at trial (for example, using real-time transcription of witnesses' trial testimony to display during the attorney's closing)

KEY TERMS	
animations and GCI re-creations	evidence or document cameras
annotation systems	Handheld Computing Devices/PDA's
barcode readers	
demonstrative boards	laptop and projector
Digital Audio Recording Device	litigation software
digital presentation	online deposition service
digital projectors	overhead projectors
digital slide projectors	Real-time Transcription/Real-time Reporting Equipment
Digital Visual Interface	
drivers	trial technology
electronic case filing	video impeachment/video deposition presentations
Enhanced Projection Systems	wireless keyboards

DISCUSSION QUESTIONS

1. Why is it essential for paralegals to be familiar with various trial technology tools and litigation software?

2. What are the various technology tools that paralegals must be familiar with?

3. What are the paralegal's roles in ensuring that trial technology and software are used in the most effective and efficient way possible in preparation for and during trial?

4. What are some "best practices" to keep in mind when dealing with trial technology and litigation software?

5. Refer back to the case of *Woodward v. WelcomeMart.*

    a. List five examples of technology tools that Patty, the plaintiffs' paralegal may use to help her attorney prepare his case and explain why they would be useful.

    b. List five examples of technology tools that Danny, the defendant's paralegal may use to help his attorney prepare his case and explain why they would be useful.

PUTTING TOGETHER A TRIAL NOTEBOOK

An organized trial notebook provides tremendous value in preparing for trial and at the trial. The task of putting one together often falls on the paralegal—this chapter focuses on tips for trial notebook assembly, organization, and maintenance.

CHAPTER OVERVIEW

By the end of this chapter, you should be familiar with

- the functions of a trial notebook;
- the sections in a typical trial notebook;
- tips for organizing a trial notebook;
- trial notebook maintenance and updates;
- the paralegal's role in putting together a trial notebook.

THE FUNCTIONS OF A TRIAL NOTEBOOK

You already know that preparation and organization is key when it comes to trial work. One of the ways to help your attorney be prepared and organized at trial is by putting together a trial notebook. Trial notebooks ensure that your attorney is able to access information efficiently and effectively at the precise time she needs it.

The trial notebook's main function is to serve as a collection of the essential information that the attorney will need at trial. It includes all important facts, the law, and expert analysis and opinion. It sets forth the trial team's strategy and organizes and synthesizes the most important information so that it can be easily utilized. It collects ideas and organizes them in a cohesive system to present information clearly, concisely, and efficiently. It also includes the attorney's expected "battles," points of clarification on any issues in contention, and support for the client's position. In essence, the trial notebook functions as the game plan for victory.

Trial notebooks can vary by attorney. Not every attorney prepares or uses a notebook; some may prefer to use several notebooks at trial. The sections of a trial notebook and the information the attorney chooses to include can also vary—not just by attorney, but also depending on the type of case that is being tried.

THE PARALEGAL'S ROLE IN PUTTING TOGETHER A TRIAL NOTEBOOK

As with many other tasks in preparing for trial, much of the paralegal's role in putting together a trial notebook has to do with organization and efficiency. The paralegal and attorney must work closely together to assemble the necessary material and organize the notebook. The goal of the notebook should be to present a quick and easy reference to the legal authority on various issues that are expected to arise during trial, to the expected witnesses and evidence at trial, and to the attorney's mental process and plans at trial. The trial notebook should help the attorney fine-tune her presentation and portray a persuasive case to the jury.

Litigation paralegals may assist by culling and gathering all of the documents, records, and information that will go into the trial notebook. For example, the paralegal may be in charge of going through a deposition and culling information that the attorney can use to cross-examine and impeach the trial witness; the paralegal may also gather records, documents, and legal research that will go into the notebook.

The paralegal will most likely be in charge of organizing the notebook as well: determining what sections the notebook should include, color-coding and cross-indexing sections, and filing documents under those sections. And finally, the paralegal may be entrusted with maintaining the trial notebook and ensuring that the trial notebook is updated, stays intact, and makes it to trial when the attorney needs it.

SECTIONS OF THE TRIAL NOTEBOOK

What goes into the trial notebook? Although every attorney will have her own way of organizing a trial notebook, there are some components that you will typically see in most notebooks. Some examples include

- Overall Strategy—this section sets out your attorney's themes and goals at trial, identifies the strengths and weaknesses of the client's case, and details the attorney's step-by-step strategy for persuading the jury.

- Opening Statements and Closing Arguments—this section includes a draft of the attorney's opening statements and expected closing arguments.

- Direct Examinations—this section includes questions for and expected answers by witnesses that the attorney will conduct a direct examination of.

- Cross Examinations—this section includes questions for witnesses that the opponent will call and your attorney will cross-examine; it also includes information about the witnesses' background and credibility, which the attorney will use to impeach those witnesses.

- Exhibits—this section includes copies of exhibits that the attorney expects to introduce at trial.

- Damages—this section details the client's damages and includes supporting information and relevant records.

- Pleadings, Prior Motions, and Rulings on Motions—this section includes copies of the pleadings, motions (such as motions for summary judgment or motions dismissing portions of the claims), and important rulings made on those motions.

- Pretrial Conference—this section details a summary of pretrial discussions and the final pretrial conference decisions.

- Jury Instructions—this section includes the proposed jury instructions that the attorney will present to the judge.

- Juror Questionnaires—this section includes questions the attorney proposes that the jury answer in advance and questions the attorney intends to ask members of the jury array during voir dire.

- Jury Panel—this section details identifying information about the jurors; for example, it may list each juror's name or number, occupation, age, education level, and family members.

- Verdict Forms—this section includes any jury verdict forms that will be given to the jury during deliberations.

- Records—this section includes copies of relevant police, medical, or other types of records in the case.

- Research—this section details relevant substantive legal research, including any statutes, case briefs, or even complete copies of important cases.

- Procedural Rules—this section lists relevant rules of procedure and evidence that are likely needed, so the attorney may refer to them during trial. Many trial attorneys have an evidence and rules of procedure book with them at the trial.

- Miscellaneous—this section includes notes and information on anything else your attorney deems important to include and have at her fingertips during the trial.

CHECKLIST 11.1: TIPS FOR ORGANIZING A TRIAL NOTEBOOK

- First, discuss with your attorney what information the attorney wants to include in the notebook, the attorney's preferred method of organizing the notebook (and ideas on what sections to use), and ways to structure the notebook so that it corresponds to the attorney's goals at trial.

- After consulting your attorney, determine what documents and records you need to gather and what information you need to cull. Come up with a plan for getting each document within a reasonable time for putting together the notebook.

- Make copies of important documents and records that will go into the notebook.

- Establish who will prepare each component and develop a timeline to review with the attorney the components of the notebook.

- Go through any other important documents that will not be reprinted in the notebook in full, but may still contain information your attorney will use at trial—for example, a deposition transcript that may be used for impeachment purposes during cross-examination. Cull the information that is relevant, and present it in writing in a concise and efficient way.

- Make a plan for organizing the notebook. Make a list of components that your attorney wants to include and determine what types of cross-indexing and color coding will be necessary. Gather the materials that you will need to organize the notebook: for example, a binder and index tabs, as well as cover sheets for each section that you may need to pre-print.

- Next, put the notebook together. Be sure that each document is filed under the proper section, that the sections are organized effectively, that documents are cross-indexed as necessary and paginated, and that the notebook is prepared in the most efficient and effective way overall.

- Double-check with your attorney to ensure that the trial notebook contains all necessary information and is organized properly, according to the attorney's preferences and specifications. Make any changes as necessary in order to keep current with changing strategies and decisions.

TRIAL NOTEBOOK MAINTENANCE

As with any other tool used by attorneys at trial, the notebook will not do you (or your attorney) much good if it is not properly maintained and secured. Paralegals are often entrusted with trial notebook maintenance and security. As part of this task, make sure the trial notebook is kept secure and updated whenever necessary, stays intact, and gets to your attorney when she needs it before or during trial.

The paralegal serves an important function in maintaining the trial notebook—in fact, trial notebook maintenance often falls solely on the litigation paralegal's shoulders. To keep your trial notebooks well-maintained, update them as necessary: when new facts come to light; when legal issues are clarified; when court rulings are handed down in your case; when you find new case law or other legal authority; and when there is a change in strategy. Maintaining the trial notebook entails inputting new information, organizing or re-organizing information as needed, and making sure that all indexes and cross-indexes are kept current and detailed. By maintaining the trial notebook, the paralegal must ensure that it is kept up-to-date factually and legally.

TABLE 11.1: PERSPECTIVES FOR THE ATTORNEY-PARALEGAL TEAM

While your attorney is working on	You might assist by . . . .
• Deciding on the format and "big picture themes" to use for the trial notebook and the presentation of the case to the jury	• Checking your firm's usual trial notebook format, as well as sample formats and checklists available • Providing an extra set of eyes and ears to the attorney on notebook planning and organization
• Deciding on the documents to include in the trial notebook	• Assembling, organizing, and coordinating the documents • Using the index and cross-index systems • Locating and organizing supporting information for trial notebook documents
• Using the notebook at trial	• Ensuring that the trial notebook is maintained and organized • Coordinating and including any additionally discovered information that the attorney wants to include in the trial notebook • Ensuring that the attorney has access to the trial notebook whenever she needs it • Overseeing back up of trial notebook documents

KEY TERMS	
closing arguments	juror questionnaires
cross-examinations	opening statements
direct examinations	themes and goals at trial
exhibits	trial notebook
impeaching the trial witness	trial notebook sections
jury array	verdict forms
jury instructions	

DISCUSSION QUESTIONS

1. In what ways are trial notebooks an important part of preparing for trial?

2. In what ways do paralegals play an important role in putting together a trial notebook? What are some typical related tasks that paralegals may be entrusted with?

3. What paralegal skills are important to putting together a great trial notebook?

4. Refer back to the case of *Woodward v. WelcomeMart.*

   a. What sections might Patty, the plaintiffs' paralegal, include in her attorney's trial notebook? What about Danny, the paralegal working for the defense?

   b. List some documents that you think might be filed under each section of Patty's and Danny's trial notebooks.

HANDLING PRETRIAL AND SETTLEMENT MATTERS AND ASSISTING WITH VOIR DIRE

This chapter details preparation tips for pretrial conferences, settlement issues, alternative dispute resolution, and putting together a settlement brochure. It also describes the paralegal's role in assisting with the jury selection process.

CHAPTER OVERVIEW

By the end of this chapter, you should be familiar with

- the paralegal's role in settlement issues;
- ways to assist your attorney with alternative dispute resolution;
- preparing for a pretrial conference;
- putting together a settlement brochure;
- the paralegal's role in the jury selection process.

ASSISTING WITH SETTLEMENT ISSUES

As you know by now, the vast majority of lawsuits are not adjudicated in court. Because so many suits are settled by the parties outside of court, it is important for litigation paralegals to be familiar with settlement issues and alternative dispute resolution.

Paralegals may assist with drafting a demand letter during the onset of a case. The demand letter presents an opportunity to explore settlement issues with the client and opponent. Oftentimes, a settlement without the expense and delay of litigation can be a win-win situation for all involved—except the attorneys who lose the benefit of hourly fees. Still, it is sometimes difficult early on for the plaintiff to lower his expectations on the promise of guaranteed money in hand today, and for the defendant to recognize that the plaintiff's claim is sufficiently meritorious to withstand the filing of dispositive motions—therefore, the parties may find that it is worth seriously discussing settling the matter.

FIGURE 12.1: SAMPLE DEMAND LETTER

Small & Mighty, P.C.
156 Elm Street
Nita Town, Nita 55555

Peter Mighty, Esq.   *(555) 123-4567*

June 25, 2008

Mr. Jamal Rodriguez
and
Softwaresells, Inc.
1600 Pennsylvania Avenue
Nita, Nita 55555

December 1, 2008

Dear Mr. Rodriguez and Softwaresells, Inc.,

This office represents Shane Condo of Hill Road in North Nita, Nita, in claims against you concerning funds and stock owed to him regarding his development of Softwaresells and revenues generated through his efforts. Demand is hereby made upon you to resolve this matter or suit will be brought in accordance with Nita General Law chapter 93A, contract law, and other pertinent legal grounds. Unless a satisfactory resolution is achieved in the next 30 days then Mr. Condo will vigorously pursue all available remedies. Please be aware that violations of Nita General Law chapter 93A provide for a recovery of two to three times the amount of actual damages plus an award of attorneys' fees.

Jamal Rodriguez approached Mr. Condo with a software application that he thought could be of value to the healthcare industry but was uncertain of its readiness or how to market it. He solicited and requested Mr. Condo's expertise on its present market readiness, its value to the market, and how to penetrate the payer sector (insurance companies such as Blue Cross Blue Shield firms, regional health plans such as Mighty Health Plans, Thrifty, Harvard Puritan, Community Health Plan, and others throughout the country).

Beginning in 2003, Jamal Rodriguez and my client met multiple times to review the software application and to pursue an arrangement whereby Mr. Condo would be compensated with commissions and equity based on the number of client contracts that he could help generate. Mr. Condo is involvement was important to the success of the venture because of his background and significant experience with evaluating software applications for the healthcare industry, his advising software vendors on market strategy, and because of his nationwide network of industry contacts developed over his then fifteen years in the business. Softwaresells used his expertise to help introduce the software to prospects and develop a strategy for penetrating the market.

In early 2005, Jamal Rodriguez, Mr. Condo, and Peter Pumpkans met to finalize the terms of the contractual arrangement. Mr. Condo's share of equity included an immediate 33% of the stock of the corporation and, consistent with his level of expertise in the industry and in marketing to the heath care industry, 50% of all profits that Softwaresells generated. Mr. Condo's percentage of stock was to increase to a maximum of 49% upon completion of securing the first three clients. All net profits were to be distributed periodically in equal amounts on a monthly or quarterly basis. It was agreed that the revenue would be held in the common bank account to fund the daily operation of the business. Jamal Rodriguez maintained the bank checking account and managed the relationship with the payroll firm that would distribute payroll distributions to contractors working for Softwaresells and to Mr. Condo and Mr. Rodriguez. Stock certificates were granted to Mr. Condo on March 1, 2005, for 33,000 shares and again on May 1, 2005, for an additional 3,000 shares as a bonus for the acquisition of Softwaresells' first client that Mr. Condo was instrumental in helping to establish.

Mr. Condo diligently worked to ensure the success of the business, providing numerous leads as well as introductions to potential clients and knowledge of how to position the software to the industry. These efforts developed into establishing at least one client and other prospects. The one client, Mighty Health Plan, generated over $800,000 in gross revenue from 2005 through 2006 and was ongoing on December 24, 2006, when Mr. Condo received notice from Softwaresells attempting to void the parties contract and revenue distribution plan. We have reason to believe that Mighty Health Plan remains an active client of Softwaresells and that the Company and Mr. Rodriguez continue to earn revenue and profits from this client from which Mr. Condo has not received compensation. Mr. Condo provided numerous leads as well as introductions.

Mr. Rodriguez and Mr. Condo had agreed, based on the advice of their accountant, on a profit sharing distribution plan that provided for all remaining company net profits to be distributed equally on December 31 of each year to avoid increased tax liability. At the time the purported termination of Mr. Condo's rights on December 24, 2006, just one week before a distribution of over $100,000 was to be made to Mr. Condo, the company had over $200,000 in cash on hand in the bank. This net profit was to be divided and distributed equally to Mr. Condo and Mr. Rodriguez. In order to avoid this obligation, as well as future distributions and stock ownership, Softwaresells, Jamal Rodriguez, and others conspired to appropriate Mr. Condo's stock and money that was rightfully due him. Said actions are violations of contract and tort law and constitute fraudulent and deceptive trade practices in violation of Nita General Law Chapter 93A.

The solid business relationship and the success of the business as a result of Mr. Condo's efforts require restoring Mr. Condo to the position he was in pursuant to the parties agreement, a proper accounting for all revenues obtained during Mr. Condo's purported ouster, and a restitution of all the funds rightfully due him, including the payment of interest on those funds.

At the minimum, as of today, this includes:

2006 Net profit sharing (50% of $250,000)	$	125,000
2006 Onetime software payment (50% 0f $40,000)	$	20,000
2007 Software license and maintenance fees (50% of $36,000)	$	18,000
2007 Net Profit from Estimated Client billings (50% of $15,000 per month)	$	90,000
2008 Software license and maintenance fees (50% of $36,000)	$	18,000
2008 Net Profit from Estimated Client billings (50% of $15,000 per month)	$	90,000
Due Shane Condo	$ 361,000	

In the event you do not restore Mr. Condo's stock in the company then demand is also hereby made upon you for compensation for 49% of the value of the company, which we value at $5,000,000. This is based upon the fact that the acquisition of the first client that Mr. Condo helped broker, Mighty Health Plan in St. Louis, increased the value of the company's net worth considerably. The business value of a software firm is measured at 5 times the annual revenue generated by the company. In 2006, Softwaresells was experiencing a run rate of revenue of $1 million plus. This would place a value on Mr. Condo's 49% as being worth $2,450,000.

We would welcome sitting down with you in an effort to resolve this matter or mediating this dispute. From both a legal and business standpoint there is no reason to needlessly waste money on attorneys' fees. In the event you do not respond to this demand within 30 days then Mr. Condo intends to pursue vigorously all available remedies.

Thank you for your anticipated cooperation.

Very Truly Yours,

Peter Mighty

Paralegals can play an essential part in the settlement process. The paralegal may ensure that proper documentation and support exists for the claims and defenses and is readily available to support the attorney's arguments on the value of the claim for settlement purposes. The paralegal may also serve as the conduit for information between the clients and attorneys.

Paralegals provide needed support to the attorney throughout the settlement process. While trial attorneys conduct settlement discussions on their clients' behalf, paralegals may assist with fact gathering and verification, computation of damages, correspondence, and client comfort.

A paralegal may also help the attorney put together a settlement brochure or settlement workup: a document for the other side that summarizes all of the major facts supporting the client's case and damages. The purpose of the settlement brochure is to encourage the other side to resolve the case out of court—this is a persuasive document that should present the client's side of the story in a convincing manner.

CHECKLIST 12.1: PUTTING TOGETHER A SETTLEMENT BROCHURE

Some considerations that may arise with this paralegal task include:

- Ensuring that all of the facts that will be included in the settlement workup are verified with the client;

- Listing the client's personal information or company background;

- Describing properly the client's damages that were suffered or will be suffered in the future;

- Describing properly the client's other damages, including covered damages, actual expenses, and general or nonpecuniary damages;

- Verifying the client's actual expenses to date and collecting all necessary documents;

- Giving a detailed description of the events from the client's point of view;

- Verifying the client's story through witnesses, documents, and any other evidence that is available, and using the most important points to support your client's position regarding settlement;

- Investigating further facts to include in the settlement brochure;

- Laying out all the information in a readable, persuasive, and professional brochure;

- Making arrangements for printing and obtaining the brochure.

ASSISTING WITH ALTERNATIVE DISPUTE RESOLUTION

Paralegals can also provide valuable assistance during alternative dispute resolution. Because it is a faster, more economical, and often more amicable method of resolving disputes when compared with litigation, alternative dispute resolution is now often the favored method of dispute resolution.

Some typical tasks that paralegals may be involved with during alternative dispute resolution include

- Assisting the attorney with researching and choosing a skilled mediator with experience in your client's type of case, or a neutral third party to conduct alternative dispute resolution, such as a conciliator;

- Assisting your attorney by researching the qualifications and suitability of various arbitrators;

- Researching the ADR providers' prior decisions, if available, and discussing prior decisions of the ADR providers with attorneys who have presented cases to them;

- Scheduling dates for alternative dispute resolution meetings;

- Obtaining any consent forms necessary;

- Verifying the facts of the client's story with the client, witnesses, documents, and any other sources of information;

- Verifying the client's damages;

- Writing a summary of the client's case that will be presented to the ADR provider;

- Assisting the attorney with presenting the client's story in the most convincing and persuasive light.

PRETRIAL CONFERENCES

Pretrial conferences are used by the court to manage the litigation and trial of the matter. The court generally orders the attorneys, and sometimes the parties, to appear for one or more pretrial conferences in order to expedite the disposition of the action, establish control of the case, improve the quality of the trial through proper preparation, and to facilitate a settlement. Many cases will have an early pretrial conference shortly after the case is filed to deal with scheduling matters, the extent of discovery, and needed motions and a final pretrial conference scheduled after discovery.

As the case gets closer to the trial date established during the initial pretrial conference, many courts will order a final pretrial conference. Some of the reasons for the conference include

- discussing the possibility of settlement;

- simplifying the issues;

- eliminating frivolous claims or defenses;

- amending the pleadings if necessary or desirable;

- obtaining admissions and stipulations about facts and documents;

- ruling in advance on the admissibility of evidence;

- avoiding unnecessary proof and cumulative evidence;

- identifying trial witnesses and pre-numbering exhibits that will be used at trial;

- identifying the questions that will be submitted to the jury; and

- establishing a reasonable limit on the time allowed to present evidence at trial.

You will need to review all essential information with your attorney well before the final pretrial conference. Cases are won through thorough, proper preparation for the final pretrial conference; conversely, they are lost through poor preparation for it. Well in advance of the final pretrial conference, discuss with your attorney what specifically he wants you to research or prepare and what additional information he needs you to obtain in order to have a successful final pretrial conference.

THE PARALEGAL'S ROLE IN THE JURY SELECTION PROCESS

Voir dire is the process by which lawyers question potential jurors to determine their fitness and suitability to serve on the jury. Lawyers use voir dire to develop a relationship with jurors; to elicit information from jurors, including information regarding possible bias or favoritism; to educate jurors on the issues from their client's perspective; and to find the jurors who are most likely to find in their client's favor.

Help your attorney develop voir dire questions that cannot be answered with a simple yes or no. Your goal in helping attorneys prepare these questions is to get jurors to talk about themselves, their experiences, and their likes and dislikes. Prepare the questions so the tone of voir dire is conversational, not inquisitorial. Based on the juror's education, experience, background, and opinions, will this juror likely view your client's case favorably or unfavorably? Can the potential juror empathize with your client's situation, or is he or she more likely to see the world through the other side's eyes?

Avoid writing questions that encourage jurors to look good. Because most of us believe we are fair people—or at least want others to believe it—we tell people that we will be fair during trial. Therefore, no one is likely to say that she is biased when asked, "Do you have any biases that would preclude you from being fair in this case?" Instead, ask questions designed to elicit a narrative explanation of an event that gives you insight into biases that the witness may harbor.

For example:

- When probing a potential juror about racial bias, the attorney may ask: "Some people have never gone to school or worked with a black person; could you briefly tell us about a favorable experience you may have had with someone of color?"

- When probing a potential juror about bias against awarding a large judgment, the attorney may ask: "Some people feel that it is difficult to award someone lots of money for something that happens to him or her. Under what circumstances do you think it's appropriate to award someone a large amount of money for something that happens to them?"

- When probing a potential juror about bias against awarding damages for mental suffering, the attorney may ask: "Under what circumstances do you think it is just for someone to receive money for mental injuries as opposed to physical, observable injuries?"

- When probing a potential juror about a host of potential biases, the attorney may ask: "If the judge instructs you that the law requires you as a juror to determine something in accordance with the law, would you do so even if that is contrary to your personal beliefs?"

Some jurisdictions allow individual questioning of jurors, while other jurisdictions restrict questioning to a group format. The paralegal must research and discuss with the attorney which format is in use in the jurisdiction where the case is going to trial. You can then help your attorney prepare the questions for the greatest interaction with potential jurors and the maximum benefit for your case.

TABLE 12.1: PERSPECTIVES FOR THE ATTORNEY-PARALEGAL TEAM

While your attorney is working on	You might assist by . . . .
• Preparing for a settlement conference	• Gathering financial and other supporting documents to justify settlement demands or offers • Assembling key evidence to be used during the conference (such as demonstrative exhibits designed to persuade the opponent to settle) • Researching and finding dispositive or on-point case law for legal issues • Assembling evidence to demonstrate the other side's risks of going to trial (such as prior jury verdict analyses, settlements, and demonstrative exhibits supporting your attorney's readiness to try the case)

• Conducting the settlement conference	• Helping to locate and provide information that's helpful to support the attorney's arguments • Assisting with the presentation of documents and other evidence
• Keeping the client abreast of settlement negotiations and terms	• Facilitating the attorney's contact with the client • Providing information to the client (but never legal advice!) as you are instructed by the attorney • Drafting the settlement agreement, any standard forms, and releases
• Preparing for the pretrial conference	• Researching and coordinating facts and support for the pretrial memorandum • Drafting the pretrial memorandum • If a joint pretrial memorandum is required, coordinating drafting and revisions with the other side
• Preparing for voir dire	• Drafting questions, both in paper form and oral follow-up questions • Researching any applicable local rules
• Conducting voir dire	• Making notes while the attorney is asking questions, paying close attention to jurors' body language and reactions to specific questions • Meeting with the attorney during voir dire to relay your notes and serve as a sounding board

KEY TERMS	
alternative dispute resolution	settlement
demand letter	settlement brochure
jury questionnaires	settlement discussions
pretrial conference	voir dire

DISCUSSION QUESTIONS

1. In what ways are paralegals an integral part of the settlement process and alternative dispute resolution?

2. What specific skills do you think a paralegal should possess to help facilitate settlement of a case?

3. What specific skills should you work on developing to better assist your attorney with ADR?

4. Refer back to the case of *Woodward v. WelcomeMart*.

   a. What information may Patty, the plaintiffs' paralegal, include in the settlement brochure?

   b. What questions may attorneys for the two sides ask potential jurors during voir dire in this case?

   c. What specific steps should Patty and Danny take in getting the case ready for the pretrial conference?

13

ORGANIZING A WAR ROOM AND TIPS FOR DOCUMENT MAINTENANCE

This chapter provides advice on setting up a war room, whether in the office or on location.

CHAPTER OVERVIEW

By the end of this chapter, you should be familiar with

- the benefits of a well-organized war room;
- tips for organizing the war room;
- effective document maintenance and retrieval tips;
- tips for setting up a war room on location;
- the paralegal's role in setting up and organizing a war room;
- the paralegal's role in creating an efficient document retrieval system.

THE BENEFITS OF A WELL-ORGANIZED WAR ROOM

A well-organized document retrieval system is not all you need to make your trial run smoothly: for most attorney-paralegal teams, it is also essential to have a war room—a place to store deposition transcripts, discovery documents, legal research, and any other information about the trial in an organized and easy-to-retrieve manner. Like a trial notebook, a well-organized war room can make the trial lawyer's job easier. The war room is not only the central artery for the trial materials, but also often the place for the trial team to work together and strategize. So, this space must not only project organization and maintenance, but also be a comfortable place where your trial team will actually want to stay and work.

As with any other task that entails the organization and maintenance of trial prep materials, setting up the war room is often the paralegal's job. That job starts with obtaining information about the type and size of workspace that will be needed and discussing that information with those responsible for using the space and making arrangements to lease or get access to the space. A well-prepared litigation paralegal will understand the importance of keeping all materials in one central location, maintaining a system of organization before and during the trial, and providing a principal place for the trial team to work.

PICKING YOUR SPACE

The first step to a well-organized war room is finding the right space to use. Whether you are in the office or on location, the right room, office, or corner can make a big difference in how well-controlled your trial materials will stay. In any trial or group project, efficiency is often vital to achieving the desired goal. In trials, efficiency not only equates to money, but also makes for less stress and anxiety. And it all begins with a well-organized document retrieval system, which in turn begins with the right space to store materials.

CHECKLIST 13.1: PICKING THE RIGHT SPACE FOR YOUR WAR ROOM

General questions

- Is there ample space and organization for computer equipment, desk space, and files?

- Is the space easily accessible by the entire trial team?

- Does the trial team need additional private workspaces outside the war room to prepare witnesses or have confidential discussions with clients?

- Can you fit all necessary furniture, equipment, and supplies?

- Are you paying continued attention to space concerns as the trial goes on?

- Are "creature comfort items" such as a refrigerator for cold drinks or a coffee maker needed to help speed productivity?

Organization questions

- Does the space make it easy to implement a consistent and thorough method of organizing and tracking materials?

- Are both hard- and soft-copy materials organized in such a way that they are cross-referenced to one another?

- Is material organized in multiple ways in order to give the trial team several means of finding each piece of information, thus making it easier to locate?

- Is there a separate "hot docs" category for documents that are used frequently by the trial team?

- Does the space provide you with a way to easily maintain files and keep them organized?

- Who will be the person at the end of each day to ensure that the space is kept organized for maximum efficiency?

Security questions

- How will the war room's contents be kept secure?

- Have you provided all authorized trial team members with access to the war room and security codes for electronic access?

- Who will be the war room librarian or person responsible for keeping the war room secure and accounting for any missing documents?

Technical questions

- Can the war room house all necessary equipment?

- Are there enough electrical outlets?

- Does the war room have necessary phone lines and high-speed access lines?

SETTING UP A WAR ROOM ON LOCATION

The challenges of setting up a war room are amplified if you have to establish one away from your main office: you are faced with an unfamiliar environment, sometimes traveling to distant states; you have to do much of the planning from a distance; and you often have to work very quickly to have the war room operational when you get to the location of the trial. Still, having an organized and convenient place to store all of your materials is even more important when setting up the war room on location, where your trial team will not have the familiar services or equipment of your office handy.

CHECKLIST 13.2: SPECIAL CONSIDERATIONS FOR SETTING UP A WAR ROOM ON LOCATION

- Familiarize yourself with the location and nearby services ahead of time.

- Decide on the best space for your war room: will a secure conference room in cocounsel's offices be your best bet; should you set up in a separate space in your hotel; or should you obtain temporary turnkey office suites?

- Get a layout of the space ahead of time and review its features with your attorney for the attorney's approval.

- Pay attention to your war room's proximity to other pertinent places, such as the courthouse, key service providers, or your hotel.

- Decide which materials and documents you will be shipping ahead of time and which ones you will be bringing. Make appropriate arrangements with an overnight shipping company to get material to the location and then have it returned when the trial is over.

- Never ship or take your only copies of anything with you! Members of the trial team should always be able to retrieve material in a number of different ways. You must scan all war room documents into a manageable database for ease of retrieval, and then back up all of that information at the main office as well as to an external portable secure drive. Depending on the size of the case and volume of materials, all materials often will remain accessible at your main office.

- Make sure your war room is secure, with access limited to members of your trial team only. If information is removed from the room, you must know who has it.

- Arrange for all necessary equipment, furniture, and other materials to be set up and in working order in the war room before your team arrives.

- Bring extra everything, whether it is rulebooks and file folders or simply tape and ink for the printer—the last thing you want to do is run around town searching for supplies in the middle of a trial.

- Before you leave for trial, put together a contact list for the following vendors and resources on location: copying services; stenographers; exhibit preparation services; staffing agencies; hotels and restaurants; pharmacies; dry cleaners; and any other services that your trial team may require. Create a map with these resources shown and distribute to members of the trial team.

- Also have your attorney review and approve for distribution a contact list of everyone on the trial team. The contact list should contain each person's name, cell phone number, home phone number, e-mail address, IM address, and any other pertinent contact information. You should circulate the list electronically as well as hand it to the trial team on laminated, wallet-sized cards.

- Consider deadlines, cost, and any other limitations to setting up your war room, but do establish your war room to maximize efficiency. Do not scrimp and save a few bucks on something that will later cause the attorneys lost time or aggravation.

- Check with your attorney and the rest of the trial team about any special war room requests. Trial attorneys all have their quirks—you are not going to change them; your job is to accommodate them. You must be familiar with the needs and preferences of your trial team and anticipate those needs ahead of time.

- Don't underestimate the importance of accounting for all possible glitches. When the attorney needs something for trial, no excuse will suffice—in fact, some might tell you that if you cannot locate something, your best bet is to drop on the floor and feign a heart attack (which is, incidentally, the same thing you may wish for when you face the attorney's wrath for the document that is still missing!) To avoid theatrics, you must anticipate the worst and plan for mistakes.

TABLE 13.1: PERSPECTIVES FOR THE ATTORNEY-PARALEGAL TEAM

While your attorney is working on	You might assist by . . . .
• Deciding where to set up the war room	• Securing and coordinating a safe and adequate location for the war room • If setting up the war room outside of the firm or on location, coordinating in advance the location of the war room and ensuring that the space is adequate
• Deciding on the technology and features that need to be included in the war room	• Coordinating the technology that will be needed • Coordinating, copying, and assembling the documents that will be included • Arranging for the equipment, technology, furniture, and other materials that need to be included • Making sure the war room has adequate supplies • Organizing and setting up the war room

| • Using the war room | • Monitoring the trial team's use of the war room and ensuring that the war room stays organized |
| | • Keeping the war room up-to-date, stocked with supplies, and secure |

KEY TERMS	
cross-index document retrieval system "hot docs" category	setting up on location war room war room librarian

DISCUSSION QUESTIONS

1. What are the paralegal's roles, duties, and responsibilities in setting up a war room?

2. What special considerations might arise when setting up a war room on location?

3. Refer back to the fictional case of *Woodward v. WelcomeMart.*

    a. How should Patty, the paralegal working for the plaintiff's attorney, structure her war room? What documents should she include in the war room? What method of organization should she use?

    b. How about Danny, the paralegal working for the defense—in what ways do your answers to the questions above change if the war room is being organized in Danny's office?

PART III
WORKING TOGETHER

14

WORKING WITH YOUR ATTORNEY

How can the attorney-paralegal team best work together in preparation for and during trial? Paralegals will find valuable tips for working together with their attorneys in this chapter.

CHAPTER OVERVIEW

After reading this chapter, you should be familiar with

- tasks that attorneys assign to their paralegals before and during trial;

- the importance of collaboration between the attorney and paralegal;

- tips for working together with your attorney;

- tips for strengthening the attorney-paralegal team.

By now, you understand that paralegals perform integral practical functions as part of the attorney's preparation for trial; you also know that paralegals must be familiar with the substantive and procedural rules that govern the trial process. But there is one more key component to assisting your attorney efficiently and effectively: working together as the attorney-paralegal team.

Consider the following twenty "commandments" for working together with your attorney:

1. **Cooperate.** You should always strive for cooperation and collaboration with your attorney. For example, arrive early to work or offer to stay late and work with the attorney whenever a case requires you to, rather than running out of the office at 5:00 p.m. on the dot. Working together as a team will make for more efficient and effective trial preparation.

2. **Collaborate.** You should keep the lines of communication open between you and your attorney. Do not assume that you know what the attorney is thinking—or vice versa. When things are the craziest, say, "How is it that I can help you get done what needs to be done?" Don't just wait for a task to be assigned. Keep the dialogue between you and the attorney going to make your team stronger and more effective.

3. **Strategize.** You should ensure that you fully understand and know your attorney's goals and strategies before and at trial. For instance, before you call the copy shop to place an order, ask the attorney whether there are any copies of exhibits he or she would like you to order in color. Ideally, you should discuss with your attorney any new task that you are entrusted with to see how the task—and your work—fits into your attorney's trial prep strategy.

4. **Coordinate.** You should ensure that your plans and workload correspond to your attorney's plans and workload before and at trial. If you are not on the same page as your attorney, your team will not be effective at planning and conducting litigation. For example, after you've finished a discovery-related task that the attorney assigned to you, ask the attorney what you can work on next. Understand what your attorney needs from you—for everything the attorney does, you should be familiar with the corresponding paralegal tasks that you need to do to facilitate your attorney's job.

5. **Anticipate.** You should anticipate your attorney's needs at trial. Whether it is extra copies of exhibits, last-minute research, or witness coordination, things may pop up during the trial that your attorney will need your immediate help with. Take extra supplies and copies with you to trial. Make your job (and your attorney's) as easy as possible by accounting for your attorney's needs at trial before you get to the courtroom.

6. **Organize.** You should assist your attorney with organization in preparation for and during trial. Have a checklist ready for every paralegal task in preparing for trial, and keep to your checklists. From the trial notebook to the war room to electronically stored information, your attorney is counting on you to keep things organized, thereby ensuring efficiency and productivity.

7. **Stay efficient.** You should strive for efficiency in preparation for trial and during trial. For example, anticipate what documents the attorney will need to conduct a deposition, put them together early, and make sure the attorney has them in an organized format at the deposition. Perhaps the most important way litigation paralegals can assist their attorneys in preparation for trial is by increasing the attorney-paralegal team's efficiency.

8. **Research.** You should hone your research skills and assist effectively in research tasks. Find legal authority for that new case that the attorney intends to file on behalf of a new client. From legal research to fact-gathering and factual investigation, the paralegal's involvement is essential.

9. **Maintain files.** You should assist your attorney with case and file maintenance. Paralegals are often in charge of setting up and maintaining new files, both electronically and in hard-copy form. Master the skills you need to ensure that your attorney's files stay organized, secure, and easy to retrieve. There are five words that every busy trial attorney likes to hear: "I know where that is."

10. **Keep secure.** You should assist your attorney with keeping the case secure. For example, ensure that the contents of the trial notebook and war room are secure at all times and their contents are accounted for and properly overseen by you. Protecting confidentiality is essential, and the paralegal can play a big part.

11. **Observe.** You should serve as your attorney's extra set of eyes and ears. For example, you can help by observing a witness's behavior for credibility or looking out for a witness's arrival to court. The paralegal is often entrusted with observing the things that a busy attorney cannot.

12. **Meet deadlines.** You should stay productive, meet deadlines, and handle your share of the workload. Trials are busy, and they are often fraught with time crunches, stress, and deadlines (some of them cropping up at the last minute). For instance, you can play a key role in a case by obtaining that last-minute exhibit that the attorney needs for his or her trial presentation. Better your time management skills to make the most of the time you have on the job, thereby increasing your attorney's productivity.

13. **Stay current.** You should keep up-to-date on relevant rules, technology, and trial preparation methods and tools. Technology and the law have something in common: they can both change quickly, sometimes from one day to the next. You should strive to keep up-to-date in your role as a paralegal, so you can ensure that your attorney is up-to-date on both legal and technical issues. One way to stay current is by reading relevant books, trade journals, and other publications.

14. **Assist.** You should assist your attorney with coordinating the witnesses, exhibits, and documents that will be presented at trial. For example, you may be the person in charge of coordinating witnesses and exhibits. Whatever tasks are assigned to you, make efficient use of your time when it comes to assistance at trial.

15. **Understand.** You should understand the work of your attorney, as well as any constraints on your attorney. Paralegals must be familiar with the daily work of their attorneys, and they must also understand any boundaries that the attorney must keep in order to tailor the paralegal's own work to the attorney. For example, you have to be familiar with the rules of ethics, any budgetary or time constraints, and any strategy considerations that may be a part in the attorney's approach before and during trial.

16. **Serve your purpose.** You should be clear about your job responsibilities and how your work fits into trial preparation. Understand the tasks you are there to do (as well as the tasks that should be left up to your attorney) and the purpose and roles you serve as a member of the trial team. For instance, you may be entrusted with interviewing the client during intake, though you should never give the client legal advice about the client's case.

17. **Seek guidance.** You should be willing and able to ask your attorney for guidance whenever you need it. It is essential that you know whom you can turn to if

you have questions or need assistance on the job. For example, if you are handling a type of case with which you are not familiar, seek out the advice of a more experienced paralegal or other legal professional about some of the key tasks and checklists you can anticipate. Do not assume that you can figure out the answers when you are not entirely sure of the correct thing to do or say; ask for help.

18. **Seek training.** You should request training when you need it, seek out training on your own, and keep up with your training through continuing education and professional development opportunities. For example, you can find training and professional development opportunities through paralegal associations, paralegal schools, bar associations, and other groups for legal professionals. Also take advantage of any training opportunities that your firm or attorney offers.

19. **Seek evaluation.** You should seek to be evaluated periodically, and ask your attorney about areas in which you can improve your work. Request a periodic evaluation, asking the attorney about your strengths and weaknesses. You should also conduct periodic self-evaluations and keep track of your professional accomplishments and goals.

20. **Stay professional.** You should aim to have a professional and pleasant relationship with your attorney—as with any relationship, the "Golden Rule" applies to the attorney-paralegal team. Even when trial preparation becomes stressful or you encounter a difficult client, strive to keep your cool. Stay courteous, clear, and professional—doing so will help you establish a positive reputation in the legal field.

By keeping these twenty tips in mind, you can work towards strengthening your professional relationship with your attorney, which will ultimately make the attorney-paralegal team stronger when it comes to trial preparation. Remember: effective and efficient trial preparation requires that the attorney and paralegal work together as a team.

Q: How can litigation paralegals best work together with their supervising attorneys?

A: Answer by Anita Haworth, litigation paralegal at Campbell Kyle Proffit and President of the National Federation of Paralegal Associations

You must absolutely be flexible, able to juggle multiple tasks at one time (without getting them all mixed up), patient, detail-oriented, and organized . . . . A paralegal needs to be sure that the work product is accurate, timely, and complete. He/she must be willing to go beyond the obvious and look for the next step. In other words, you don't just do the minimum—you try to anticipate what is needed next and get it done. Further, you must always do your best. The way to succeed here is to anticipate what needs to be done next and then go ahead and do it without having to be asked. In addition, you must be tuned in to the fact that not every case needs to be handled the same way, so you must be cognizant of when and how things will be different . . . . Pay attention to the particular attorney, get to know his/her preferences, and then be sure to provide him/her with the work product that is in the format he/she wants. Make sure that it is thorough and concise. We definitely have a team concept here. Paralegals are assigned to particular attorneys, and then I work with that attorney on nearly every type of case he/she takes. Our attorneys do tend to "specialize" in particular types of cases though, so I tend to have more knowledge about those types of cases than others.

A: Answer by Julie D. Hunt, Litigation Paralegal at Saladino, Oakes & Schaaf, PLLC in Paducah, Kentucky and the 2006 American Association for Justice Paralegal of the Year

It takes time and competency to be an integral part of the litigation team. This is what we should all strive for; this is the purpose of a litigation paralegal. I don't see how you can be an effective litigation paralegal without being an integral part of the team. How do I know I am an integral part of the team? Mr. Oakes simply does not go to trial without me. When I was named the Paralegal of the Year by the American Trial Lawyers Association, we were scheduled to be in trial the same time as the presentation in Seattle . . . . I was not able to accept the award in Seattle. Fortunately, they shipped my award, and I was able to go to the next ATLA convention in South Beach.

KEY TERMS	
anticipating your attorney's needs at trial	collaboration
	cooperation
attorney-paralegal team	functioning as a team

DISCUSSION QUESTIONS

1. Why is it essential for the attorney and paralegal to function as a team when preparing for trial?

2. In what ways can paralegals ensure that they collaborate with their attorneys?

3. Refer back to the *Woodward v. WelcomeMart* case.

   a. In what ways did paralegals Patty and Danny work as a team with their respective attorneys?

   b. What examples of collaboration did you read about in that chapter?

   c. Which examples would you adopt on the job as a paralegal?

   d. What, if anything, would you do differently than Patty and Danny in order to ensure that you are working as a team with your attorney?

WORKING WITH OTHERS

This chapter will provide helpful advice for working with opposing counsel, clients, the courts, and others involved in the litigation process.

CHAPTER OVERVIEW

By the end of this chapter, you should be familiar with

- the paralegal's role in working and interacting with clients;
- tips for interacting with clients;
- working with the courts;
- working with opposing counsel.

WORKING WITH CLIENTS

The rule about staying courteous, clear, and professional at all times does not just apply to working with your attorney. In fact, that rule is perhaps even more important when it comes to working with others outside the attorney-paralegal team. After all, as the paralegal, you are an extension of the attorney; the image you project, the way you interact with others, and the professional reputation you establish all have a bearing on how others see your attorney and your team—not just you!

Paralegals are important in various ways when it comes to interacting and working with clients. For example, paralegals may

- serve as the main point of contact between the attorney and the client;
- be the first person who interviews the client about his case;
- be entrusted with coordinating the case with the client—for example, ensuring that the client attends the trial or provides necessary documentation and information;
- be in charge of collecting documents, records, and other evidence from the client;

- need to communicate important information to the client and keep the client abreast of important deadlines;

- play the role of "hand-holder," helping the client work through difficult situations and providing a sympathetic ear in which to vent;

- have to observe the client and how the client responds to requests for information to help the attorney assess the client's credibility.

CHECKLIST 15.1: TIPS FOR INTERACTING WITH CLIENTS

- Be clear, both when giving information to the client and when seeking information from the client. Make sure the client understands the information you are providing or need from them.

- Do not give legal advice! Legal advice constitutes the practice of law, which is something that must be reserved for your attorney. (See more about this in Chapter 18.) If you are in doubt about the types of questions you may answer or the information you may provide to clients, you must always discuss it with your attorney before divulging.

- Understand your role in client contact—get clear guidelines from your attorney and be clear about the ways in which you should interact with clients and the boundaries you need to establish and keep between clients and yourself.

- Relay important information to your attorney. Remember that part of the paralegal's role is to facilitate interaction and communication between the attorney and the client.

- Manage unrealistic client expectations from the beginning—and discuss them with your attorney. It is imperative to discuss these issues with your attorney as soon as there is indication that the client expects something that she isn't likely to obtain.

- Stay courteous and professional, even in the face of clients who are venting, angry, or upset. You will undoubtedly experience your fair share of difficult clients: the client who is frustrated with the length of time his case is taking; the client who knows the law better than anyone; the client who distrusts lawyers or the legal system; and the client who is dishonest. Part of your job as a legal professional is to stay courteous even when dealing with these difficult clients.

Working with the Courts

Litigation paralegals will find themselves interacting with court personnel on the job, too—for example, the paralegal may need the court clerk's help with docketing a deadline, filing a document, obtaining information, or finding the answer to a question about the case.

Checklist 15.2: Tips for Interacting with Court Personnel

- Be as specific as possible when you are looking for information, assistance, or guidance.

- Know the court's makeup and organization to understand whom you need to turn to with various questions.

- Before you call or go to the courthouse, make sure you have everything you need to bring with you (necessary documents, docket numbers, or filing fees, for example) in order to help the court personnel help you better.

- Turn to your trial court for guidance on legal questions and even legal research—many, if not most, trial courts have law librarians who can assist and guide you in the right direction if you need help with a research project.

- Do not ever assume that you do not need to be pleasant to a court employee just because he or she is not a judge. Not all court personnel may have the power to rule on your client's case, but most have the ability to help you when you need information, guidance, or assistance. Establishing a strong and professional working relationship with your local court personnel is essential to doing your job well. The three-part rule about being courteous, clear, and professional applies to working with court personnel as much as anyone else.

Working with Opposing Counsel

Most of the communication between opposing counsel and your firm will likely be done by your attorney. Still, there are some times when you might find yourself calling opposing counsel's offices—for example, to schedule a meeting or ask a simple question at your attorney's instruction.

CHECKLIST 15.3: TIPS FOR INTERACTING WITH OPPOSING COUNSEL

- Talk to your attorney before you approach opposing counsel.

- Be careful! Understand the scope of your role and the limitations on the information you can provide to or seek from opposing counsel. Also be familiar with any ethical issues that may arise—and ways to avoid them—when dealing with opposing counsel.

- Again, be absolutely unambiguous about what you are seeking from or need to provide to opposing counsel.

- Follow up conversations in writing. If you have just scheduled a meeting, send a follow-up letter to opposing counsel and make sure you provide your attorney with a copy of the letter to keep the attorney informed of the status of the matter. If you are asked to provide opposing counsel with something, note deadlines and details in writing. Also keep your attorney apprised of any communications you have with opposing counsel.

- Remember to stay clear, courteous, and professional, and to conduct yourself in a manner that is in sync with the reputation you're seeking to establish for yourself. Today's opposing counsel may mean tomorrow's job offer!

KEY TERMS	
boundaries	facilitating interactions
client expectations	follow-up letter
collecting documents	legal advice
courteous, clear, and professional	legal professional
deadlines	opposing counsel
ethical issues	unambiguous

DISCUSSION QUESTIONS

1. Who are some key players with whom litigation paralegals have to maintain contact and work together? In what ways are paralegals essential to working with others outside their own firms?

2. What are the three key things to effectively working with others that the paralegal must always employ?

3. Refer back to the case of *Woodward v. WelcomeMart.* Consider the following situations in which paralegals Patty and Danny may have to interact and work with others outside their own firms—how should they handle those interactions? What examples of "right" versus "wrong" conduct can you think of in each interaction? What advice would you give to the paralegal in each example about interacting with others?

   a. Patty needs to obtain medical records of Christopher Woodward, and Christopher will need to sign a release in order for Patty to receive them.

   b. Danny's attorney, who is busy at trial on another matter, has asked him to call the plaintiffs' attorney to request a thirty-day extension to file the answer to the complaint.

   c. Patty receives an angry telephone call from Christopher Woodward, who is complaining about having to get more information and saying that he feels the case is just being dragged out.

   d. Danny needs to have the client sign an affidavit that his attorney has prepared.

   e. Patty needs to schedule a deposition with the WelcomeMart manager, and she needs to check with the other side regarding the manager's times of availability.

   f. Patty needs scheduling information from a clerk who works for the court in which the case was filed.

BEYOND THE PARALEGAL TITLE

Trial prep does not just fall on paralegals—from e-discovery specialists to practice group leaders, from trial graphics preparers to litigation consultants, many non-lawyers provide valuable help to trial attorneys. This chapter provides information about working with other non-attorneys who assist with trial prep.

CHAPTER OVERVIEW

By the end of this chapter, you should be familiar with

- various non-attorney legal staff who may be hired by your firm to assist with trial preparation;

- the roles and purposes of those nonlawyer staff at the firm;

- the ways that other nonlawyer staff can assist the litigation paralegal in the process of preparing for trial;

- tips for working with non-attorney legal staff.

At many firms, the litigation paralegal will not be the only support staff assisting the attorney with preparing for trial. Some firms, particularly midsized and larger ones have a whole slew of people with different job titles who are working on various aspects of a case or overseeing firm operations. Your team does not just include the attorney and the paralegal. The litigation paralegal must be able to cooperate, collaborate, and communicate well with other nonlawyers at the firm to ensure maximum efficiency and effective trial preparation.

Here are just some of the other people you may meet on the job—and some useful tips for working together with them:

Other Paralegals

Their Roles at the Firm: Let's start with the obvious: at many firms, you will not be the only paralegal on the job, though some small firms and sole practitioners may have just a one-person support staff. Paralegals work in many settings: law firms, corporate law departments, legal aid offices, and the government, just to name a few. Some paralegals specialize and work in a specific practice area—like business law or family law—while others may be generalists. Paralegals typically assist attorneys with substantive legal tasks, like research, investigation, and preparation for trial.

Ways They Can Help You in Trial Prep: They can make you more efficient: chances are, they have "been there, done that," particularly if they have more experience. They can offer you helpful tips on anything from working with a particular opposing counsel to getting in contact with the most trusted outside providers in other cities. They can also give you substantive help—if you are unsure about how to draft a particular pleading, for example, you can ask a more experienced paralegal for her tips.

Legal Secretaries/Administrative Assistants

Their Roles at the Firm: While paralegals are more likely to handle substantive projects in preparation for trial (such as research, interviewing, or fact gathering), legal secretaries are more likely to work on clerical tasks. A legal secretary, for example, may take care of filing or typing. It is important to note that there is not always a clear division of substantive and clerical tasks among paralegals and legal secretaries. Many paralegals—particularly those at small firms—also take care of clerical work; conversely, a capable employee may be called a legal secretary but still perform "paralegal tasks," such as meeting with clients or drafting correspondence. In fact, the title "legal assistant" does not mean the same thing from one firm to another: some firms use it to refer to their paralegals, while it is what others call their legal secretaries.

Ways They Can Help You in Trial Prep: They may assist you with some clerical and even some substantive tasks, like document preparation and imaging and travel arrangements and scheduling. They can also offer you vast institutional knowledge, particularly if they have been at the firm longer than you—they may know whom to turn to at the firm if you have a particular question; and they may also have an archive of information and resources that they can let you access.

Paralegal Managers or Supervisors

Their Roles at the Firm: Paralegal managers are in charge of overseeing the work of paralegals, as well as paralegal hiring, firing, and training. Some firms have in place paralegal hierarchies: you may start out as a junior or entry-level paralegal and work your way up to a more senior position, and your work may be supervised by a paralegal manager in addition to your attorney.

Ways They Can Help You in Trial Prep: They can review and supervise your work; offer you guidance and answers to your questions; and they may steer you towards resources and training opportunities. They may serve as your general contact when you have a question or issue at work—whether it is difficulties with case management or difficulties working with another paralegal.

Office Managers

Their Roles at the Firm: The office manager may be in charge of the firm's day-to-day operations, such as billing and overhead, ordering supplies, and overseeing human resources. At some firms, the role of office manager may be filled by a capable paralegal—a sole practitioner, for example, may hire just one support staff, whose roles may range from paralegal duties to taking care of the firm's day-to-day operations. Conversely, at some larger firms, the office manager's duties may be shared by several people: one may be in charge of billing and bookkeeping, for example, while another may focus specifically on human resources.

Ways They Can Help You in Trial Prep: They may offer you help, support, and resources with office supplies, budgeting, and scheduling.

Business Managers

Their Roles at the Firm: While the office manager may take care of everyday operations, the firm's business manager may be in charge of long-term business projections: business development, budgeting, getting new clients, and the like. Think of law firm business managers as C-level executives; they may even be non-practicing lawyers or lawyers at the firm who oversee the firm's business in addition to their case load.

Ways They Can Help You in Trial Prep: They may offer you help and support with budgeting, billing, and timekeeping issues.

Receptionists

Their Roles at the Firm: The firm receptionist is generally the first person with whom clients and others outside the firm come into contact—so he is the "face" of the firm in many ways. Typical receptionist job responsibilities include answering phones and taking messages, greeting visitors, and generally ensuring that the firm projects a great first impression to clients and others.

Ways They Can Help You in Trial Prep: By being cordial and pleasant to your client, witnesses, and others involved in the case, they can play a big part in making everyone comfortable with the firm and its work. They may also offer you help with some clerical tasks.

Practice Group Managers

Their Roles at the Firm: A practice group (a term typically used by larger firms) refers to a group of lawyers who concentrate in a particular practice area, such as litigation or corporate law. The practice group manager oversees the group's work and operations: for example, she may ensure that work is flowing in the right direction; that every member of the practice group (including the paralegals) is doing his job correctly; and that every member of the group is properly trained and kept up-to-date.

Ways They Can Help You in Trial Prep: Besides your attorney, this person is most likely your boss. She likely oversees case management and everything that goes into preparing for trial. The practice group manager can assist you if a major problem should arise—though with most questions, you should probably approach your attorney first.

Legal Investigators

Their Roles at the Firm: Legal investigators assist attorneys with fact gathering, record gathering, record checks, background checks, and witness interviews, to name a few tasks. Some legal investigators may provide additional services, such as service of process. Attorneys typically hire investigators on a case-by-case basis as independent contractors. In many cases, the paralegal may work closely with the investigator; in others, the paralegal may be in charge of investigation entirely.

Ways They Can Help You in Trial Prep: They can assist you with a slew of projects: investigation, fact-gathering, interviews, record gathering, witness locating, skip-tracing (trying to find a missing person), and serving process, just to name some.

Legal IT Specialists

Their Roles at the Firm: Legal IT specialists assist attorneys with technology: they may manage the firm's technological equipment; answer technical questions and assist with trouble-shooting; and help the attorney implement new equipment, technology, and software. From docketing to litigation software, legal IT specialists take care of the firm's technical needs.

Ways They Can Help You in Trial Prep: They can help you with the technical side of trials: setting up databases and database management; assisting with trial technology; ensuring that the programs you need to prepare for trial are running seamlessly; and helping you solve those problems that your computer always seems to have at the worst times!

Law Librarian

Their Roles at the Firm: Law librarians assist attorneys with research projects, whether electronically or hard copy. The firm may also have a librarian in-house to maintain the firm's library and online databases, as well as to assist attorneys and others at the firm who need to find answers to legal research questions.

Ways They Can Help You in Trial Prep: They can help you perform legal research and update your research, as well as navigate the many different sources of legal authority, both electronically or hard copy. They can assist you with finding sample forms and other secondary sources that will help you learn how to do your job well. They can also keep you informed: they can alert you to new cases and other sources that matter to your case if you keep them in the loop regarding what interests you.

Litigation Consultants

Their Roles at the Firm: Litigation or trial consultants assist attorneys with trial strategy, planning, and presentation. They may assist the attorney with everything from jury selection and formulating voir dire questions to "translating" the attorney's argument into a winning presentation that the jury can understand and relate to. Litigation consultants will typically be hired by the firm as outside independent contractors.

Ways They Can Help You in Trial Prep: Depending on the budget, they can assist the firm on basic issues like assisting with voir dire or be full-fledged trial preparation partners, helping you with case strategy and everything that goes into preparing for trial. They can assist your attorney with evaluating the attorney's presentation and the jury's likely reception and verdict.

Litigation Prep Providers

Their Roles at the Firm: Litigation or trial preparation providers can assist the attorney with a whole host of services: trial graphics, "day-in-the-life" videos, electronic discovery management, file and document management, exhibit preparation, stenography services, and deposition transcript digesting, just to name a few. Litigation prep providers may specialize in a specific area of trial preparation or may be generalists, and they are typically hired by the firm as outside independent contractors.

Ways They Can Help You in Trial Prep: Depending on the budget and your case, they can assist you with many different services, from software to exhibits to e-discovery.

Legal Marketers

Their Roles at the Firm: Legal marketers may be in charge of various projects: they handle public and media relations; oversee marketing and cross-marketing efforts; and assist attorneys with business development projects. A legal marketer's role at the firm is to put the firm in the best possible light and market the attorneys' professional services to potential and existing clients.

Ways They Can Help You in Trial Prep: They can offer you knowledge and expertise on trial publicity; take media requests; directly interact with the media and the public throughout the trial; and direct the media (within ethical boundaries, of course) to specific story lines that will hopefully place your case in the best light.

CHECKLIST 16.1: TIPS FOR INTERACTING WITH OTHER STAFF

- As always, be courteous, clear, and professional. Whether you are dealing with the attorney who manages your practice group or the receptionist who takes down your messages, basic politeness, respect, and courtesy matter.

- Learn to see every member of your firm (yourself included!) as a member of the professional team. When it comes to trial preparation, teamwork matters.

- Ask for help and ideas—for example, take a more experienced paralegal out to coffee and pick her brain about substantive tips and ideas for handling your projects. Make sure you do this at a time when the other person is not pressed in her own work, and stay professional even if the other person does not appear sufficiently interested. Offer the same help when another staff member needs it.

- Make your requests timely and courteous. For example, if you need to request a travel allowance from your office manager, be sure you give him enough time, follow office procedures, and act polite.

- The same goes for outside providers—schedule things with sufficient lead time, and offer clear directions as to how you would like things to be done. Check in from time to time, and coordinate with the provider to ensure that you are all on the same page.

- Become familiar with any hierarchies that are in place at your firm—and follow protocol! At most firms, both attorneys and legal staff will fit into some hierarchy: associates may be supervised by partners, while paralegals may be supervised by managers. You should understand how the hierarchy operates, and you should know whom to turn to with various questions.

On a final note, it is important to mention that different firms assign different titles to their various non-attorney legal staff employees and contractors—so a nonlawyer's job responsibilities may vary by firm, even though she has a particular title. When you begin working with another nonlawyer, ask your colleague to detail his job responsibilities at the outset and consult with your colleague about mutual expectations and ways to best work together. And if you are applying for a non-attorney legal staff position, be sure you are clear about the job's duties and requirements.

Q: Why is continuing legal education important, and how can paralegals ensure they receive proper training and keep up-to-date?

A: Answer by Janet A. Sullivan, Senior Paraprofessional Manager at Reed Smith, LLP and Beth Weller, Paraprofessional Coordinator at Reed Smith, LLP

Today's paralegals need to keep up with the changing legal rules and procedures, court cases, and technologies. They should also take advantage of any learning opportunities (formal as well as informal) that come their way. In the current legal and economic environment, they need to be willing to expand their comfort zone and get involved in new areas and be willing to take on new challenges . . . . Our firm has created Reed Smith University ("RSU"), which offers all sorts of in-house education classes and training in technical, legal, and professional development topics that the paralegals are encouraged to attend. We also provide training on Lexis and Westlaw as well as various litigation software programs and databases. Our firm is very proactive when it comes to training programs. We are asked for our input as to what we, the paraprofessionals, would like to see offered through RSU. We work diligently with the administrative manager of the RSU program to create programs of interest to the paraprofessionals.

A: Answer by Julie D. Hunt, Litigation Paralegal at Saladino, Oakes & Schaaf, PLLC in Paducah, Kentucky and the American Association for Justice's 2006 Paralegal of the Year

I highly recommend the NALA [National Association of Legal Assistants] programs. I find them to be state of the art and easy to follow.

A: Answer by Anita Haworth, litigation paralegal at Campbell Kyle Proffit and President of the National Federation of Paralegal Associations

Education gives you the basic knowledge, whereas experience (and working with great attorneys) gives you the confidence to know what is important and what is not. The firm pays for me to attend CLEs and the ABA Tech Show. In addition, I have purchased books, and the firm reimbursed me for them.

KEY TERMS	
business manager	litigation prep provider
legal assistant	non-attorney legal staff
legal investigator	office manager
legal IT specialist	paralegal
legal marketer	paralegal manager
legal secretary	practice group manager
litigation consultant	

DISCUSSION QUESTIONS

1. Who are some of the non-attorney legal staff who can assist litigation paralegals in trial preparation? In what ways can they assist the paralegal?

2. What tips would you offer for interacting with non-attorney legal staff at your firm?

3. Refer back to the case of *Woodward v. WelcomeMart*. Consider the following projects with which Patty and Danny need help. For each project, identify the non-attorney legal professional to whom Patty or Danny should turn, as well as tips for working with that person:

   a. Patty needs to find a federal statute.

   b. Danny needs to find a public record.

   c. Patty needs to enlarge a document that her attorney will present as an exhibit at trial.

   d. Danny is experiencing a problem with his laptop.

   e. Patty noticed a discrepancy in her time sheets.

   f. Danny is having difficulty working with another paralegal on his team.

   g. Patty lost a phone message from a client.

   h. Danny is unfamiliar with and untrained on a task that his attorney asked him to do.

HANDLING THE HEAT

Trials come with plenty of stress; this chapter offers tips for time, stress, and temper management.

CHAPTER OVERVIEW

By the end of this chapter you should be familiar with

- avoiding time-wasting practices in preparation for trial;
- practical ways to manage time and increase efficiency;
- tips for stress management during trial preparation;
- avoiding some of the sources of frustration that come with trial preparation;
- avoiding combustible behavior that can occur in trial preparation.

Litigation comes with a lot of heat. Trial preparation and trials entail a lot of stress and frustration; last-minute projects and problems arise; and the process can bring out the worst in people—whether it is the client, opposing counsel, or a member of your trial team. To be successful on the job as a litigation paralegal, you must be able to manage your time, your temper, and your job-related frustrations effectively. To put it simply, you must be able to handle the heat.

COMMON SOURCES OF FRUSTRATIONS DURING TRIAL PREP

There are several sources of stress and frustrations that can make your job as a litigation paralegal harder. Here are some examples:

- The client. Clients can become distrustful, less than forthright, unpleasant, and even abusive; they can be less than responsive to your requests for information; and co-clients can even stop speaking to each other in the middle of the trial—for example, if one client wants to settle but the other does not.

- Witnesses. As an example, a witness can get lost on her way to trial, leaving you scrambling not only to locate the witness, but also to assist your attorney with finding other evidence or testimony to produce at trial while you are awaiting the witness.

- The case you have prepared. For example, a piece of evidence you have prepared may become more important than anticipated—perhaps because your attorney notices that the jury appears to be paying particular attention to issues that originally seemed less important.

- The judge. Your team may encounter unexpected or even unsupported rulings by the judge.

- Your own trial team. You may have a team member who is not pulling his weight, does not work well with others, fails to perform the task that he was asked to do, becomes the team's "weak link" and crumbles under pressure, or has difficult "pet peeves" that the rest of the team must be able to handle.

- Opposing counsel. Unfortunately, you will encounter opposing counsel who "forgets" that she orally agreed to the introduction of certain evidence without the keeper of the records having to be present, or agreed to take an important witness out of order because of the witness's vacation schedule.

Handling those types of frustrations can be stressful, and maintaining professionalism under such circumstances can be taxing. Any one of those stressors can make you less effective, less efficient, and make your job more unpleasant. Here are some techniques to help you deal with the frustrating side of trials.

CHECKLIST 17.1: TIPS FOR DEALING WITH TRIAL PREP FRUSTRATIONS

- Anticipate. Recognize that trials come with frustrations, that nothing ever goes perfectly, and that the worst things can happen at the most inopportune times. Make sure you have a plan in place for handling some of the common stressors in preparation for trial.

- Know your team. You should understand the environment and circumstances under which each team member performs best—and the circumstances that can make them crumble under pressure. Understand each person's limits, pet peeves, and the best way to resolve conflicts.

- Stay respectful. Control your own temper and use your words judiciously, even when you are faced with someone else's combustible behavior.

- De-stress. Periodically, do whatever it takes to escape the stress that comes with trial prep, whether it is eating or exercise. Keeping your mind, body, and soul healthy will allow you to deal better with the pressures that come with the job.

- Have a support network in place, both at work and outside of the office. You need to have people to rely on when things happen, whether it is the office manager who can mediate conflict or your partner at home who can get the kids to bed after soccer practice.

- Carry your weight! This is important: you must stay productive, meet deadlines, and do what is expected of you. (You probably need to be prepared to carry a portion of other people's loads as well. It may not be fair, but you need to expect the worst of people.)

COMMON TIME-WASTING PRACTICES IN TRIAL PREPARATION AND AT TRIAL

When it comes to litigation, there is never enough time. In any case, staying productive and efficient, doing what is expected of you, and saving time on various paralegal tasks can make you a much more effective paralegal. But there are some time-wasting pitfalls you must avoid.

Here are some common examples of time-wasting practices:

- Not doing a task right the first time. When you have to do it more than once, you are wasting precious time.

- Not delegating. The team loses out when the "wrong" person is put on a task and that person's time could be better spent elsewhere.

- Not being able to locate things. Trial teams spend countless hours searching for stuff, whether it is that important deposition transcript or that great case that works well in the attorney's argument but cannot be located when it is needed.

- Not using the most efficient tools at your disposal. If you are not taking advantage of technology, software, research tools, and outside provider services that can make your job more efficient, you are probably losing your team valuable time and money.

- Simply put: procrastinating, not pulling your weight, and not performing as efficiently and productively as you can.

CHECKLIST 17.2: TIME MANAGEMENT TIPS FOR LITIGATION PARALEGALS

- Plan, prepare, and allocate more time to each task than you think you will need. Expect that the witness will get lost and need additional time and make alternative plans; expect that the only copy of the exhibit you need will disappear, and make extra copies. Always give yourself extra time, and always be ready to have to answer to your team or your client more quickly than you may originally anticipate.

- Take your time, but do things right the first time rather than having to go back and re-do them.

- Learn to compartmentalize different tasks and then to prioritize those tasks in order of immediate importance. If the trial notebook needs to be organized at the same time a client needs your attention, you must be able to quickly figure out who you should turn to first.

- Have realistic expectations. Litigation at times requires long schedules, late nights, and weekends. You should recognize the demands on your time that you will face if you decide to work as a litigation paralegal.

- Delegate tasks whenever possible. Each person on the trial team should aim to assist the attorney with the substantive tasks that best fit his expertise. The most efficient trial teams know how to delegate work to the right people.

- Aim for redundancy in your databases, indexes, and files. Index and cross-index each document—you should be able to search and find files in several different ways and under several different search terms.

- Use time-saving tools that can help you increase your efficiency. Whether it is a computer program that can help you find files faster or an outside provider who can save you valuable time on exhibit preparation, invest in tools that can increase your team's efficiency in the long run.

- Learn not to waste other people's time. Do not always tell your outside provider that your project is due immediately if it is not; that way, when you have a real emergency, you can count on your provider to get you what you need as soon as possible.

- Anticipate the worst—and plan for it accordingly.

- Stay productive! You cannot be efficient without meeting deadlines, doing the work that is expected of you, and pulling your weight.

KEY TERMS	
anticipate	redundancy
combustible behavior	respectful
delegating	stress
de-stress	timeline
frustrations	time management
procrastinating	unsupported rulings
realistic expectations	"weak link"

DISCUSSION QUESTIONS

1. What are some of the most common sources of stress and frustration during trial preparation, and how can paralegals avoid them?

2. What are some common time-wasting practices in trial preparation? How can litigation paralegals master time management skills that will allow them to become more efficient?

3. Refer back to the case of *Woodward v. WelcomeMart.* How should paralegals Patty and Danny handle the following situations:

   a. It is the night before an important deposition, and Patty's witness has not made travel arrangements yet.

   b. Danny's attorney is irate: he cannot find an important deposition digest.

   c. The Woodwards are in a major disagreement about the case.

   d. Danny's fellow paralegal was supposed to pull two important cases for Danny two days ago, and Danny still has not received them.

   e. The judge in the case has ruled that some of the damages cannot be recovered due to the statute of limitations; Patty's team was not expecting this ruling.

   f. Danny is experiencing anxiety and chest pains whenever he sits down to work on the Woodward case.

A PRIMER ON PARALEGAL ETHICS

This chapter provides a brief overview of legal ethics for litigation paralegals.

CHAPTER OVERVIEW

By the end of this chapter, you should be familiar with

- the professional responsibility rules that govern attorneys' conduct;
- ethics rules governing attorneys' supervision of paralegals and other non-lawyers in the law office;
- rules on client confidentiality;
- rules on conflicts of interest;
- laws governing the unauthorized practice of law;
- the paralegal's role and involvement in helping the attorney comply with ethics rules.

ETHICS OVERVIEW

To be able to assist their attorneys effectively, paralegals must understand the ethical considerations that may arise before and during trial. Ethics refer to codes of conduct or standards of behavior to which members of a profession must adhere. Attorneys are bound by ethics rules that are imposed by their respective supreme courts, regulatory agencies, or state bar associations. In order to practice law, attorneys must typically graduate law school, pass a bar exam, pass a character and fitness analysis, be sworn in as attorneys, and in some states become a member of their state's bar association. During the process of becoming a member, attorneys pledge to uphold various ethics rules adopted by the state's supreme court.

Lawyers are often a self-policing profession: either the state has a regulatory agency dominated by attorneys that oversees the conduct of lawyers in that state, or a state bar association will have a division made up of bar counsel whose job is to oversee attorneys' conduct. If an attorney is accused of professional misconduct, she may be investigated by bar counsel and brought up on charges. Breaking the ethics rules can result in serious sanctions for the attorney, including fines, public and private reprimands, term of suspension or indefinite suspension, and even disbarment, where the attorney's license to practice law is taken away.

Most states' codes of ethics are found in the court rules and follow the Model Rules of Professional Conduct (MRPC,) promulgated by the American Bar Association.

THE PARALEGAL'S ROLE

Attorneys are governed by ethics rules—paralegals are not. Because nonlawyers in the law office are not currently licensed or regulated—with the exception of some regulation of Legal Document Preparers and others by the state of California—there are no licenses for paralegals to obtain and no ethics rules for them to follow. A paralegal will not be suspended or disbarred if he fails to comply with the ethics rules.

Still, the paralegal's attorney may be sanctioned not only for her own misconduct, but also misconduct committed by the paralegal whom the attorney is in charge of supervising. So, the paralegal's role in ethics is really to assist the attorney with ethics compliance. Paralegals do this in two ways: by making sure their own conduct is ethical, and by helping the attorney make ethical choices. While your license may not be on the line if you do something unethical, your attorney's may be—and ultimately, that means your job may be on the line as well.

CLIENT CONFIDENTIALITY

One of the most important ethics rules deals with client confidentiality. Rule 1.6 of the MRPC makes it clear that an attorney must not reveal the confidences of his client unless the client consents to the disclosure, or unless another exception applies in your jurisdiction—for example, the lawyer reasonably believes that the client is likely to commit a criminal or fraudulent act that will cause death or serious bodily harm to someone else.

From the paralegal's perspective, you must make sure that you do not inadvertently disclose confidential information. Consider the following examples, all of which represent potential breaches of confidentiality:

- Sharing the identity of your client with your spouse;

- Sharing details about an ongoing case with other paralegals at a networking event;

- Leaving a client file open on your desk where others can walk by and glance at the file's contents;

- Leaving an interoffice memo open on your computer where others can walk by and glance at the memo's contents;

- Inadvertently including confidential information in materials that others outside of your firm will see—such as the paralegal who included snippets of a confidential attorney-client phone call in an exhibit she prepared for trial.[1]

- Inadvertently faxing or e-mailing the wrong document to someone outside of your firm.

- Taking a phone call from one client while you have another client in your office waiting for a meeting with the attorney.

It is not hard to see how quickly and easily an inadvertent disclosure of confidential information can happen. As a result, you have to take precautions to ensure it will not happen. First, check with your attorney before talking about a client or a case to anyone outside of your law firm. Also, make sure you keep files, client documents, and any other materials containing confidential information organized and protected.

Conflicts of Interest

Conflicts of interest make up another important part of the ethics rules. A conflict of interest refers to any situation where the attorney is "serving two masters" and derives from the law of agency—as the attorney is the agent of the client, the attorney continues to have a duty of loyalty to the client even after the representation ends.

Though the most common form of a conflict of interest is where an attorney represents a new client in a case where the opponent is a former client of the firm, conflicts of interests do not end at "former client–present adversary" situations. Anything can be a conflict of interest, as long as it requires the attorney to serve some interest other than the client's.

The following are all examples of conflicts of interest:

- Representing the plaintiff in a negligence case against a defendant who is a former client of the firm;

- Representing the wife in a business transaction where the firm originally represented the husband in his divorce from the wife;

- Representing both husband and wife in an amicable divorce;

- Representing both buyer and lender in a real estate transaction;

---

1. Georgetown Manor, Inc. v. Ethan Allen, Inc., 753 F. Supp. 936 (S.D. Fla. 1991).

- Accepting a bequest from a client from an estate you worked on;

- Conducting a business deal with a client, such as buying the client's house;

- Having sex with a client or someone else related to the case—such as one paralegal who had an affair with the husband of a client that the firm was representing in divorce proceedings![2]

- Having a personal bias against a client;

- Hiring a new employee (lawyer or nonlawyer) who previously worked for opposing counsel in a case the firm is now handling—like in one case where the court ruled that the firm had to be disqualified from a case due to a new paralegal hire who used to work for opposing counsel.[3]

That last example is particularly important. All lateral hires—those who have worked for another firm previously—can "taint" their new firms, whether they are lawyers or nonlawyers. So, a paralegal could bring a conflict of interest into her new law firm. As a result, law firms must perform routine conflicts checks whenever the firm gets a new client, new matter, or new hire. Conflicts checks involve a thorough analysis of the firm's database to investigate whether any potential conflicts of interest are found.

If a conflict of interest arises, the firm must take precautionary measures to ensure that its representation of the client will not be compromised. The client may consent to the conflict of interest (in some cases, a writing is required). Some firms will build a "Chinese wall" around the employee who has the conflict; this means the employee will not work on the case, nor have any contact with files and other materials in the case. Still, in serious conflicts of interest, the conflict may be imputed to the entire firm, and the firm may be disqualified from representing the client.

PROPER SUPERVISION OF THE PARALEGAL'S WORK BY THE ATTORNEY

Rule 5.3 of the MRPC makes it clear that attorneys must supervise the work of their paralegals and other nonlawyer assistants. Moreover, the supervision rule holds the attorney responsible for the paralegal's misconduct if the attorney ordered the misconduct, knew about and ratified the misconduct, or failed to remedy or mitigate the nonlawyer's misconduct.

From the paralegal's perspective, you have to be vigilant about requesting adequate training, supervision, and guidance. Law firms and attorneys get busy; paralegals get entrusted with important tasks; and it can be easy for an attorney to trust his or her paralegal so much that the attorney fails to provide proper supervision as required under the rules. Consider the following examples:

---

2. Logan v. Hyatt Legal Plans, Inc., 874 S.W. 2d 548 (Mo. 1994).
3. Latson v. Blanchard, No. 18867, 1998 Ohio App. LEXIS 4619 (Sept. 30, 1998).

- You draft an important letter to a client. Your attorney declines to read the letter, signs it, and tells you to send it out anyway.

- You draft a pleading. Your attorney only cursorily glances at the pleading, signs it, and tells you to file it.

- You interview a new client. Your attorney never talks with the client—instead, the attorney relies entirely on your notes to prepare and file a pleading on the client's behalf.

All of the above are examples of lack of close supervision by the attorney that are warning signs of potential trouble down the road. In fact, the attorneys in these hypothetical situations are likely breaching other ethics rules as well as the supervision rule. Remember: as a paralegal, everything you do has to be directly supervised by your attorney.

Laws on the Unauthorized Practice of Law

In order to practice law, one must have a law license. If a person practices law without a license, he is engaged in the unauthorized practice of law (UPL). UPL is serious business: most states impose criminal penalties—including fines and jail time—on those who are found guilty of practicing law without a license. In addition, many state bar associations' ethics rules prohibit attorneys from assisting someone in UPL.

Just what constitutes the practice of law depends on the definition used by the courts in your jurisdiction. Many courts and ethics experts describe the practice of law as any of the following: establishing the attorney-client relationship (including setting fees); representing a client in court (including filing any court documents on the client's behalf); or providing legal advice, which means not just reciting the law, but applying the law to the client's specific facts and situation.

Tasks that fall under any of the above categories must be left up to the attorney; should a paralegal engage in any of them, she would likely be practicing law without a license. Consider this—all of the following people are potentially breaking the law:

- A paralegal who drafts and signs a complaint on behalf of a client, with no attorney supervision;

- A paralegal who tells a potential client that the attorney typically charges $1,000 for the kind of transaction that the client needs help with—all fee discussions should be between the attorney and client;

- A paralegal who advises a neighbor that the statute of limitations on a potential case that the neighbor wants to file is three years.

Another important consideration here lies in representing yourself as a paralegal. Though attorneys might understand who paralegals are and what they can and cannot do, the general public may not. You may encounter clients and others who think a paralegal can do pretty much everything the lawyer can, including give legal advice and answer legal questions. It is imperative that you make it clear to clients that you are not an attorney and cannot give them legal advice. It is also important that you represent yourself as a nonlawyer in all of your dealings at the firm—for example, courts have ruled that paralegals can have business cards and be listed on firm letterhead and in firm directories, but their nonlawyer status must be clearly apparent in all of those.

The bottom line: do not take chances by performing a task that could be viewed as the unauthorized practice of law. UPL is a three-letter word with which you do not want to become familiar!

OTHER IMPORTANT ETHICS RULES

Competence

Rule 1.1 of the MRPC says that an attorney must competently represent his clients. Competence refers to having the requisite knowledge and skill necessary to properly assist the client with her case. From the paralegal's perspective, you must not accept any tasks that you do not know how to do or do not feel comfortable doing, unless you will receive adequate training and guidance to help you perform the task.

Diligence

Rule 1.3 of the MRPC requires attorneys to act with reasonable diligence and promptness and to zealously represent their clients. In addition, Rule 3.2 requires attorneys to take reasonable measures to expedite litigation. Rule 1.4 also requires the lawyer to keep a client reasonably informed about the status of the client's matter and to promptly comply with reasonable requests for information.

To the litigation paralegal, this boils down to several things: meeting deadlines, turning in work on time, getting back to clients on questions, and not unduly delaying the client's case. It goes without saying that the deadlines imposed by your local court rules must be met—so if you have twenty days from service of process to file your defendant's answer, you cannot file it a day late and think it will suffice. But diligence and promptness also extends to your professional relationship with the client: both lawyer and paralegal must generally avoid procrastination that may adversely affect the client's case.

Safekeeping Property

Rule 1.15 of the MRPC says that attorneys must keep client property separate from property that belongs to the attorney or firm. This includes personal property, of course, but also client funds—money belonging to a client must be kept separate from the firm's finances. From the paralegal's perspective, if you are entrusted with money, checks, or invoices at the firm, be sure your attorney gives you clear guidelines.

Interacting with the Court and Opposing Counsel

Rule 3.3 of the MRPC requires candor towards the court: an attorney may not make a false statement of law or material fact to the court, fail to disclose a material fact or controlling legal authority to the court, or offer any other evidence that is false. Rule 3.4 also requires the attorney to act in fairness to the opposing party and counsel.

From the paralegal's perspective, this means you have to obtain and organize information so the attorney can present factual and legal authority honestly and fairly, both to the court and to your opponent. As you perform factual and legal research, for example, you must make sure you are collecting and relaying information clearly and accurately.

Solicitation

Rule 7.3 of the MRPC guards against lawyers improperly soliciting professional employment in person from potential clients. Paralegals must be keenly aware of the rule against improper solicitation, and under no circumstances should they themselves engage in solicitation of professional employment. This includes blatantly unethical conduct (serving as a "runner" who lines up cases for an unscrupulous attorney) and less obvious violations (convincing your neighbor to choose your attorney for help on her personal injury claim).

Litigation paralegals must ensure they comply with the ethics rules that govern attorneys. Remember: potential misconduct by the paralegal not only reflects negatively on the professional reputation of the attorney and firm, but may also lead to ethics sanctions for the attorney, as well as civil liability—in some cases, even criminal charges—for both the attorney and paralegal.

KEY TERMS	
competence	Model Rules of Professional Conduct
confidentiality	practice of law
conflict of interest	safekeeping property
conflicts check	state bar associations
diligence	supervision rule
ethics	unauthorized practice of law

DISCUSSION QUESTIONS

1. What are some litigation assistantship tasks where paralegals should be keenly aware of potential ethical concerns?

2. Suppose you represent the plaintiff in a medical malpractice suit. Discuss whether any of the following may present a potential conflict of interest. If so, how should your firm proceed? What are some of the potential ramifications if your firm doesn't handle the conflict?

   a. A legal secretary in your office is a patient of the defendant doctor.

   b. The firm previously represented the plaintiff's mother in an automobile accident.

   c. The firm previously represented the defendant doctor's wife in her divorce from the defendant.

   d. One of the partners in your firm is involved in a business transaction with the defendant doctor, though neither the doctor nor the partner is represented by the firm.

   e. One of the partners in your firm regularly plays golf with the defendant doctor.

INDEX

References are to page numbers.

∽

The NITA Foundation

supports NITA's core values of excellence, ethics, mentoring, inclusiveness, justice, and philanthropy through our various programs. We strive to give back to our global community by supporting the work of attorneys engaged in the representation of the underserved, indigent, and disenfranchised. To learn more about NITA's publications, programs, or the work of our Foundation, please visit us online at www.nitafoundation.org or by calling (877) 648-2632.

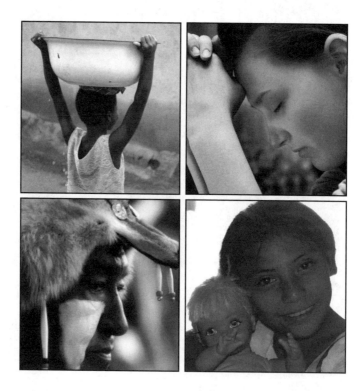

The NITA Foundation